LIEUT.-GENERAL SIR A. J. GODLEY, K.C.B., K.C.M.G.
Commanding XVII. Corps and N.Z. Expeditionary Forces.

Regimental History
OF
New Zealand Cyclist Corps
IN
The Great War
1914-1918

BY OFFICERS

To the Memory
of the
Officers and Men
of the
New Zealand Cyclists who
gave their lives in
the Great War
1914-1918

FOREWORD.

I desire to place on record my high appreciation of the good service done since the formation of the Cyclist Battalion in July, 1916, to the signing of the Armistice.

Your Battalion has had a most varied experience and few units in the B.E.F. have rendered valuable service in so many different directions or in conjunction with so many different formations.

Its work has included traffic control, the felling of trees, cable burying, repairing of trenches, the holding as Infantry of sections of the front line, the reconnaissance of front areas and the participation in offensives as advanced Mounted Troops.

The work of burying cables 6, 7 and 8 feet deep, running up to the front line in shell swept areas, and most of it done by night, proved as valuable and successful as it was arduous and dangerous. . Latterly the Battalion became so experienced and expert in this work that its personnel were employed only as supervisors.

On several occasions, when specially needed, your Battalion has done most. valuable service in the front line, both as Infantry and Mounted Troops. Of these I desire to specially mention the Battle of Messines, the filling of the gap near VIERSTRATT at a heavy cost in casualties and the holding off of the enemy for four days in April, 1918, during the critical period of the big enemy offensive. The Capture of Marfaux in the offensive of the Fifth French Army in July, 1918, and the excellent patrol and advanced reconnaissance work in the second Battle of the Somme and finally in our final advance from Arras to Mons.

I congratulate you on being selected as the only British Unit to receive a fanion from General Berthelot.

New Zealand Cyclist Corps

If Cyclists are included in the post war Army of New Zealand the traditions of your good service cannot fail to permanently stimulate both their efficiency and *esprit de Corps*.

I ask you with confidence to continue until discharged in New Zealand to do your share in maintaining the high reputation for soldierly qualities held by the N.Z.E.F.

My gratitude for your services and my best wishes for your future happiness and prosperity will follow you to New Zealand.

(Sgd.) ALEX. J. GODLEY,
Lieut.-General
Commanding N.Z. Expeditionary Forces.

XXII. Corps Headquarters,
Mons (Belgium).
6th March, 1919.

FOREWORD.

We endeavour to illustrate to our readers the actual part taken in the Great War, 1914-18, by a small Unit called the New Zealand Cyclist Corps. This Unit comprised a very small part of the N.Z.E.F., and was incorporated in the XXII. Corps Mounted Troops. Its work with this high formation separated us from the N.Z. Division (whose glorious exploits are touched upon by other writers) and naturally very little was heard in our Homeland about our doings. Casualty lists appearing in our papers here told the public that "Somewhere in France" this small Unit was kept actively employed and was striving to uphold the traditions of the British race and do its bit in the Great War.

THE WRITERS

LIEUT.-COLONEL C. H. EVANS, D.S.O.
Officer Commanding N.Z. Cyclist Battalion.

CONTENTS

CHAPTER		PAGE
I.	Formation	13
II.	On the Seas—Egypt	16
III.	Landing in France—Organisation	21
IV.	The Second Anzac Cyclist Battalion—Training	23
V.	In the Trenches	27
VI.	Training—With the Cavalry	32
VII.	Cable Laying	36
VIII.	Battle of Messines	39
IX.	The First Anniversary of the Battalion	45
X.	Gravenstrafel-Passchendale	48
XI.	Ypres	51
XII.	Enemy Offensive of March, 1918	55
XIII.	Kemmel and Meteren and Strazeele	58
XIV.	Veirstratt	61
XV.	With the French at Mont des Cats	65
XVI.	Oissy	67
XVII.	On the Marne—Marfaux	70
XVIII.	The Second Battle of the Somme	81
XIX.	Arras—Mons	91
XX.	The Armistice	104
XXI.	Our Departure from France	109
XXII.	Presentation of Fanion, Epernay	112

APPENDIX

Roll of Honour		117
Honours List		119
Nominal Roll of Original Personnel		122
Nominal Roll of Reinforcements		127

LIST OF ILLUSTRATIONS

Lieut.-General Sir A. J. Godley, K.C.B., K.C.M.G.	Frontispiece
Lieut.-Colonel C. H. Evans, D.S.O. Facing page	6
1st Cyclist Company Badge	14
The New Cyclist Corps Badge	14
The C.O. Lieut.-Colonel Evans, D.S.O.	16
Headquarters Officers' Mess	16
Officers of N.Z. Cyclist Battalion	18
Original Members ex s.s. "Mokoia," May, 1916	18
W.O.s and N.C.O.s, Headquarters and No. 1 Company	20
W.O.s and N.C.O.s of Nos. 2 and 3 Companys	20
Officers of 2nd Anzac Battalion	24
Headquarters Staff 2nd Anzac Cyclist Battalion	24
The Adjutant and his Staff	28
R.Q.M.S. and Staff	28
Areo Photo of Messines	38
Concert Celebrating First Anniversary, 1917	44
First Anniversary Dinner, 1917	44
Areo Photo of the Famous Ypres Sector	50
Lieutenant J. T. Stevens	54
Major H. D. McHugh, M.C.	64
Visit to the Front by the Prime Minister, Hon. W. F. Massey, and Sir Joseph Ward	66
Areo Photo of Marfaux	70
The Road to Marfaux	74
The British Cemetery at Marfaux	74
The Corps Guides supplied by the Battalion	78
Review of 51st Division XXII Corps	78
Dispositions of the XXII Corps, 11/11/18	92
The Battalion Flag	98
Official Entry into Mons, 15/11/18	98
O.M.R. and Cyclist's Combined Team	104
Cyclist Battalion Football Team	104
Battalion Pierrot Troupe	108
The Chateaux Baudour	108
Parade for Demobilization	110
Waiting for H.M. the King	110
The Fanion presented to the Battalion	112
The Fanion Presentation Party	114
A Captured German Cycle	114
Grave of our Adjutant, Capt. C. A. Dickeson	116
Our First Casualty—Grave of Corp. C. S. Des Barres	116
One of our Last Casualties—Grave of Private R. D. Walker	116

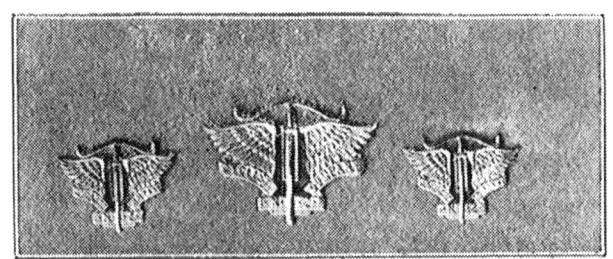

1st CYCLIST COMPANY BADGE
Issued in New Zealand.

THE NEW CYCLIST CORPS BADGE
Issued in France—with Shoulder Badges and Colour Patch.

HEADQUARTERS OFFICERS' MESS.

THE C.O., LIEUT.-COLONEL EVANS, D.S.O.

Regimental History
OF
New Zealand Cyclist Corps
IN
The Great War
1914-1918

CHAPTER I.

FORMATION.

When, on the 3rd August, 1914, the British Empire declared war on Germany, her Dominions beyond the seas answered the call and started earnestly to help the Mother Country.

In accordance with a request from the War Office, the New Zealand Government despatched a Force to Samoa on August 14th, 1914, upon the outbreak of war. On 12th August, 1914, the offer of a Voluntary Expeditionary Force for service abroad by New Zealand to the Imperial Government was accepted, and on October 16th, 1914, this Force sailed for Egypt. During the months that followed, our glorious work in Gallipoli has been told by other writers and need not be duplicated here. On 28th January, 1916, the Imperial Government suggested that in view of the large accumulation of reinforcements in Egypt, a complete New Zealand Division be formed. At the suggestion of the Army Council, details were arranged direct with General Sir William Birdwood, and the Division was formed in February, 1916, under the Command of Major-General Sir A. J. Godley, K.C.M.G., who had raised and trained the N.Z. Expeditionary Force in New Zealand, to whose leadership the whole of the subsequent brilliant success of the N.Z.E.F. is responsible.

A Cyclist Company being included in the composition of a Division, the New Zealand Government in March, 1916, offered to provide the personnel for such a Company and the offer was accepted by the Imperial Government. The officers and men of this Company were found from the Mounted Rifles reinforcements training at that time in Featherston Camp, in New Zealand, who, having more men than were necessary for immediate requirements, voluntarily transferred to this new Cyclist Company. Major C. Hellier Evans, who was in command of A Squadron, 13th Mounted Rifles, was offered and accepted the command of the Company, and the following were selected as officers :—

2nd Lieut.	G. Clark Walker	12th A.M.R.
,,	J. T. Steven	12th C.M.R.
,,	R. W. Kebbell	13th W.M.R.
,,	C. G. G. Johnson	Reserve Squadron
,,	G. L. Comer	11th C.M.R.

The establishment of a Divisional Cyclist Company was 8 officers, 196 other ranks, divided as follows :—

Company Headquarters, 2 officers   1 Major i/c.
                                           1 Captain 2nd i/c.
                                           and 13 other ranks
6 Platoons each 1 officer and 30 other ranks.

Transport consisting of 6 vehicles and 201 bicycles.

It was decided that the Company should be drawn from the Reserve Squadrons and 12th, 13th and 14th Mounted Rifle Reinforcements. Volunteers were called for on the 5th April and a selection was made ; several cycles were obtained and a riding test instituted. The Company was to leave New Zealand with the 12th Reinforcement on the 29th April, and as there was the Musketry test to be carried out and final leave to be granted, time was short. However, by dint of hard work and organisation these were carried through and as the sailing of this portion of the reinforcement was postponed for a week, it gave an opportunity to sort out the unfit and obtain organisation.

The Company, being entirely a new Unit—for Cyclists were unknown in the New Zealand Territorials—had no Mother Unit and consequently no badge. As a badge was necessary a design was submitted to the Commandant of the Camp and approved. The badge was a winged cycle front wheel and handlebars, and had on a scroll beneath the words "1st N.Z. Cyclist Company." A number were manufactured by a Wellington firm and sold to the members of the Company; free issues of badges were not made then. Shoulder titles were unobtainable, and the Unit went forward with their N.Z.M.R. titles.

The following is a list of Officers and Senior N.C.O.'s appointed:—

COMPANY HEADQUARTERS:

Company Commander, Major C. H. Evans
Company Sergt.-Major, A. P. C. Hay
Quartermaster-Sergt., F. E. Bisney
Orderly Room Sergt., A. Morrison
Artificers, Lance Corporal J. S. Hill, Private, S. C. Forrester
No. 1 Platoon, 2nd Lieut. C. G. Johnson
    Sergt. A. C. Martis
No. 2 Platoon, 2nd Lieut. G. Clark Walker
    Sergt. S. C. Fox
No. 3 Platoon, 2nd Lieut. R. W. Kebbell
    Sergt., L. H. Browne
No. 4 Platoon, 2nd Lieut. G. L. Comer
    Sergt., S. S. Ivemey
No. 5 Platoon, no officer
    Sergt., F. L. Bowron
No. 6 Platoon, 2nd Lieut. J. T. Steven
    Sergt., F. C. Matthews

The first reinforcement of 10 per cent. of other ranks was mobolised and left with the Company.

On May 2nd the Company was complete, fully equipped and paid up-to-date, and according to custom were put on active service.

The day of embarkation (6th May) approached rapidly, and on the early morning of that day the Company entrained for Wellington, where on arrival the Unit marched to King's Wharf, embarked on the "S.S. Mokoia" and were told off to sleeping quarters, mess rooms, etc.

In the afternoon the usual march through the streets of Wellington took place and the troops were given a right royal send off by the crowds of people. At 5 p.m. all were aboard and the ship cast off, amid frantic waving and cheers. Eyes became dim on realisation that they were leaving something behind—mother, sister, wife and little ones. Many a brave lad that day waved a "last farewell" to his people and Homeland.

After a quiet night in Wellington harbour the ship got under way at daylight, and so commenced our long trip to the War, at which our usefulness is recorded in other chapters.

Chapter II.

ON THE SEAS—EGYPT.

After leaving New Zealand the weather was fine for the first few days and allowed all hands to settle down comfortably in their new surroundings. Many of the men on board had never been on the ocean before, which accounted for that squirmy feeling in the region of the waistcoat. The trip across the Tasman Sea was uneventful except that a stoker who was evidently tired of life went overboard, but his desire was frustrated in a very smart and able manner by the ship's boat under Chief Officer Cordy.

The convoy (MOKOIA and NAVUA) passed through Bass Straits on the sixth day out, and after a very rough passage across the Australian Bight, arrived at our first port of call, ALBANY, on the 18th May, 1916.

The sight of land and the knowledge that once more our feet would be on *terra firma* cheered all those who had been suffering from the motion of the sea, and the prospect of a square meal hitherto denied them by Father Neptune also made the heart glad.

There were numerous things to be done; stores to replenish, water to be taken aboard, etc., and while this was being done leave was granted and nearly everyone went to the town. The townspeople treated our men most hospitably and in true Australian style made all welcome. Our departure took place on the forenoon of the 20th May, and our course shaped westward to Cape Leeuwin. After passing this Cape we ran into a heavy S.W. swell and the indifferent sailors again paid tribute to Neptune. Nearing the line the weather was finer and the temperature gradually increased. We crossed on the 31st May, and the usual ceremony of a visit from Father Neptune and his myrmidons was celebrated, the ship's crew providing the "staff." All the novices were shaved and christened, the C.O. being the first. The whole ceremony was well carried out under the watchful eye of the Master, Captain J. L. Brown, who prevented any horseplay or roughness. The weather being fine and the sea smooth, sports were frequently held, and the orchestra, under the leadership of Lieut. Carter (J. Coy., 12th Reinforcements) rendered music for our numerous concerts.

The Island of Ceylon hove in sight and we anchored in Columbo Harbour towards evening on the 4th June. Coaling was at once commenced, and it was a quaint sight to see the coolies in swarms, with next to no clothing, hard at work. Great care had to be taken of one's personal property in these ports, as these natives have a habit of claiming ownership to any detachable article they see lying about. Next day nearly all the troops were taken ashore in barges for a route march through the town, and at the Barracks were treated to "beer," such substance unknown on N.Z. Transports. Fruit was purchased cheaply, also canteen stores. We left Columbo at 6 p.m. on the 6th June, and on clearing the harbour ran into a S.W. monsoon, and for ten days steamed through storm after storm.

Land sighted again ; the east coast of Africa showed our progress, and finer weather prevailed for the rest of the voyage. Our course now took us direct for Perim Island, at the entrance to the Red Sea. The heat was now terrific, and most men discarded their clothes to the utmost limits of decency (two nurses on ship). Six days were spent travelling north in the Red Sea and our Padre gave some very interesting talks on the histories of various places passed *en route*. We arrived at Suez on the 21st June, 1916, and entered the basin the following morning, so ending our voyage. We were forty-six days travelling from Wellington, and it was said to be the record long "voyage"

Next morning, June 22nd, our ship steamed into the basin. The M.L.O. (Major Watson, A.I.R.) came

OFFICERS N.Z. CYCLIST BATTALION.

ORIGINAL MEMBERS EX S.S. "MOKOIA," MAY 1916

ON THE SEAS—EGYPT

aboard and arranged for landing the troops, stores, etc. By noon all were ashore and allotted to trains, and a little later steamed out *en route* for camp at TEL EL KEBIR.

Our impressions of Suez, representing our first introduction to Egypt, were not pleasant. The excessive heat, the dust, the dirt of evertyhing, the filthy niggers, etc., made one disinclined to linger in the uninviting spot. Of the train journey little need be said. It was mostly over desert, with occasional verdant patches where irrigation was possible. After a very hot and dusty journey we arrived at the detraining station near Tel el Kebir Camp, and were met by the Camp Staff, who conducted the Unit to Camp, where everything was in readiness.

We stayed there a fortnight, drilling in the early mornings and late at night, it being too hot to do anything by day.

Our unit was soon under orders for France. The Company was fully equipped and ready to move at short notice. 2nd Lieut. C. G. Johnston was appointed Acting Q.M. and he supervised the drawing and issue of the numerous articles of equipment required by the soldier. Leave to visit CAIRO was granted, and every member of the Company visited that quaint, wonderful and very dirty city. On 10th July orders were issued to entrain that night for ALEXANDRIA; the Company paraded and was inspected by the G.O.C Camp Area, and at 9 p.m. marched to the station and entrained, arriving at ALEXANDRIA at 5 a.m. Our transport (S.S. TUNISIAN) a well known ALLEN LINER on the Liverpool-Quebec trade (13,000 tons) was to take us across the MEDITERREAN SEA together with 800 11th Division details, some Australians, making altogether a total of 1,900. Our horses had been issued in Egypt and were sent to France a week earlier.

We sailed at 6 p.m. on our trip to MARSEILLES. Outside the harbour a small destroyer, H.M.S. "Wallflower," was waiting as our escort, and day and night throughout our trip she kept watch for submarines. The voyage was smooth and uneventful, and on Sunday evening, the 17th of July, we arrived in harbour of MARSEILLES. Arrangements for disembarkation and entraining were made, and next morning at 10 a.m. everything being aboard our train, we steamed northward to SOMEWHERE IN FRANCE.

W.O.s AND N.C.O.s, HDQRS. AND No. 1 COY.

W.O.s AND N.C.O.s OF Nos. 2 AND 3 COYS.

Chapter III.

LANDING IN FRANCE—ORGANISATION.

Throughout the day we travelled, stopping at ORANGE for lunch. Half-an-hour spell, and on again, halting near Lyons for tea, and next morning at Marcon for breakfast. These halts were at places where all troop trains stopped, and there the L of C (Lines of Communication) had boiling water ready for the making of tea. The population on the Line of Route greeted us with enthusiasm. Shouts of "*Vive* Australia" were caught up along the line. Our headgear did not appear any different to these people from our cousins over the sea; but still some more intelligent person who had evidently met the "digger" before shouted "*Vive Nouvelle-Zelande*" and though our knowledge of the French language was limited, we managed "*Vive la France.*" The small boys amused us greatly by running alongside the train shouting "Bully beef, Biscuit," the only two words they knew of the English language, but it was sufficient to fill their contract.

Our journey took us through Lyons, arriving south of Paris at midnight. The second night we skirted Paris *via* Versailles and were at EPLUCHES, EAST OF PONT OISE, for the morning meal next day; thence to AMIENS where we heard the sound of the guns for the first time on the French front, and saw numerous French soldiers, etc.; continuing through ABBEVILLE, halting at ETAPLES to drop part of our train; thence *via* Boulogne, Calais and St. Omer to Hazebrouck, where we detrained at 8.0 p.m. on the 19th July. Enquiries elicited the information that we were to go to a village called SERCUS, but nobody seemed to know exactly where it was or how far. However, we set out, and by dint of the exercise of limited French, managed to reach our destination by midnight. Progress was very slow as the men were tired and packs were heavy. We were billetted in a large farm with the 2nd Australian Division Cyclist Coy., who made us welcome and did all they could to assist us in shaking down.

Next day the C.O. (Major Evans) reported to 2nd Anzac Corps Mounted Regt. (Lieut.-Col. Long) and found that the Regiment consisted of two Squadrons, 4th Australian L.H. and a Squadron of Otago Mounted Rifles under Lieut.-Col. Grigor, D.S.O.

Major Evans then visited Lieut.-General Sir A. J. Godley, G.O.C., 2nd Anzac Corps, at LA MOTTE, and learned from him that it was intended to form a Corps Cyclist Battalion, which was to consist of New Zealand and Australian Cyclists; the present New Zealand Company was to be split into two Companies, and that two New Zealand Officers had been selected and trained in Cyclist work and would take command of the Companies. Major Evans was to command the Battalion. The Australian Company was to be reduced to one Company, *i.e.*, half of the old establishment, and the formation of the 2nd Anzac Cyclist Battalion was proceeded with. The Headquarters were to be appointed by Major Evans. The two New Zealand Companies were designated No. 1 Company and No. 2 Company.

The formation of the 2nd Anzac Cyclist Battalion broke up the original Company, and its story ends here. The subsequent history is that of a Battalion.

It must be remembered that one-third of this new Battalion was composed of Australians, and the history of the Battalion, so long as they remained with us, is the history of Australians as well as NEW ZEALANDERS.

Chapter IV.

THE SECOND ANZAC CYCLIST BATTALION—TRAINING.

On the 22nd July, 1916, in accordance with orders received from the Corps, the above Battalion came into life, the 2nd Australian Division Cyclist Company and the New Zealand Division Cyclists Company supplying the personnel. It consisted of Battalion Headquarters and three Companies, each 98 all ranks, a total of nominally 15 officers, 302 other ranks.

The following is a nominal roll of Officers and Senior N.C.O. on formation :—

    Battalion Commander, Major C. H. D. Evans (N.Z.)
    Adjutant, 2nd Lt. H. K. Love, (A.I.F.)
    Quartermaster, 2nd Lt. C. G. G. Johnson (N.Z.)
    R.S.M., R.S.M. A. C. P. Hay, (N.Z.)
    R.Q.M.S., Q.M.S. C. Forrest (A.I.F.)
    Staff Sergt., S. Sergt. A. Morrison (N.Z.)
    Signalling Sergt., Sergt. W. J. P. Ward (A.I.F.)

No. 1 Company :
    Comp. Comdr. (Tem.), 2nd Lt. J. T. Steven
    Platoon Commander, 2nd Lt. C. Clark Walker
    C.S.M., C.S.M. A. C. Martis
    C.Q.M.S., C.Q.M.S. F. E. Bisney
    Sergeants, Sergt. E. C. Fox, Sergt. L. H. Browne

No. 2 Company :
    Comp. Commander (Tem.), 2nd Lt. C. L. Comer
    Platoon Commander, 2nd Lt. R. W. Kebbell
    C.S.M., C.S.M. F. L. Bowron
    C.Q.M.S., C.Q.M.S. T. H. Dickinson
    Sergeants, Sergt. S. S. Ivemey, Sergt. H. F. Nunn, Sergt. F. C. Matthews

No. 3 Company :

    Comp. Commander, Lieut. A. E. Lord
    Platoon Commander, 2nd Lieut. P. C. Reid
    Platoon Commander, 2nd Lieut. H. J. McLennan
    Platoon Commander, 2nd Lieut. J. B. Jamieson
    Platoon Commander, 2nd Lieut. H. A. Hallenstein
    C.S.M., C.S.M. Carr
    C.Q.M.S., C.Q.M. Sergt. Gilmore
    Sergeants, Sergeant I Matthews, Sergeant Anderson,
        Sergt. McLeod.

A good deal of our time and men were employed supplying working parties at various places for the Corps, such as loading and unloading ammunition at Strazelle, traffic control on roads near by, etc.

The Company had come to Egypt without cycles, and early in August, 1916, these arrived at a railhead some distance away. Motor buses were sent by the Corps and the men went to BAC ST. MAUR, near ARMENTIERES, to draw cycles, riding them back to LA BELLE HOTESSE (the name of the village we were billetted in).

The two officers selected by Lieut.-Gen. Sir A. J. Godley, K.C.M.G., for training in Cyclist duties and drill in France, and to join the Company on its arrival, joined the Battalion at this time and were posted to command N.Z. Companies as under :—

    Captain H. D. McHugh, 3rd Battalion N.Z. (R) B, to No. 1 N.Z. Company ;
    Lieut. A. H. Richards, N.Z. Pioneer Battalion to No. 2 N.Z. Company.

The organisation being completed, training was commenced in earnest. Close order drill, Platoon training and Cyclist training being the main syllabus. Field days were held frequently, in which all branches of the Corps Mounted Troops took part. Schemes were worked on where the Cavalry, Cyclists and Motor Machine Guns

OFFICERS 2ND. ANZAC BATTALION.

Back Row.—Lt. Clark-Warker; Lt. Reid, A.I.F; Lt. Griffiths, A.I.F.; Lt. Dickeson.
Middle Row.—Lt. Steven; Lt. Johnson; Lt. Garden; Lt. Hay; Lt. Comer.
Front Row.—Lt. McLennan, A.I.F., Adjutant; Capt. McHugh, O.C. No 1 Coy.; Major Evans, C. Officer; Capt Richards, O.C. No. 2 Coy.; Lt. Lord, A.I.F., O.C. No. 3 Coy.

HEADQUARTERS STAFF, 2ND. ANZAC CYCLIST BATTALION.

played their part in the show, and each branch worked well in conjunction with the other.

A distinguishing colour patch was submitted to G.O.C. and approved of ; a white diamond 2 inches square with a red centre 1 inch, to be worn on both sleeves.

On 13th August the Battalion made its first move and route marched to a village called DOULIEU (a distance of 16 miles) where billets were secured. This move in the direction of the line was looked upon as a preliminary to some fighting and the troops became expectant. After a week in our new location orders were received to supply parties on detachment. 2nd Lieut. Comer and 30 other ranks (one Platoon) were sent to RENESCURE to be attached to the N.Z. Division Headquarters as runners and orderlies. This Platoon went with the Division to the Somme and was with it throughout the many hard and glorious battles fought by the Division. Another party of 65 O.R's under 2nd Lieut. J. T. Steven reported to Erquinghem for traffic control duties. A third party under 2nd Lieut. H. J. McLennan (A.I.F.) and 65 O.R.'s to SAILLY SUR LYS for traffic control duty.

On 2nd September orders were received from 2nd Anzac Corps that the Battalion was to move to the vicinity of BAC ST. MAUR, picking up some 100 odd details of the 1st and 2nd Australian Cyclists and the whole to be attached to the 5th Australian Division then holding the line south of FLEURBAIX and SAILLY SUR LYS. On arrival billets were found in partly ruined houses and farms abandoned by the inhabitants. The Battalion was ordered to report to 8th Australian Brigade for tactical purposes and Brig.-Gen. Tivey employed us as working parties in the front line, repairing trenches, building revetments. Our Adjutant, 2nd Lieut. H. K. Love, was transferred to the 60th Battalion A.I.F., and left us about this time, much to our regret as he was a hard worker. It is interesting to note that from the 60th Battalion, Lieut. Love was transferred to the Australian Flying Corps, received his "flying ticket," and eventually was shot down, being taken prisoner by the enemy, in whose custody he remained until the end of the War.

Chapter V.

IN THE TRENCHES.

After two weeks of the work recorded in previous chapter the Battalion was attached to the 14th Australian Brigade for duty as front-line troops, and marched from their present billets to FLEURBAIX where we were attached to the 55th A.I.F. Battalion, commanded by Major Cowey.

Nos. 2 and 3 Companies were sent into the front line and No. 1 Company took over a post at CROIX MARECHAL. The front line companies were distributed among the Australian companies and did not take over a separate Sector. The Sector was known as the BOUTILLERIE Sector and was just opposite FROMELLES, where the 5th A.I.F. Division made their attack on the 17th July. The avenues of approach were WATLING STREET, Boutillerie Avenue; TIN BARN AVENUE. Battalion Headquarters were at FORAY House, 500 yards from the front line.

I might mention here, to be more explicit to my readers, that the trenches at the front were generally made into three lines, namely (1) the Front Line; (2) the first Support Line, anything from 50 yards to 300 yds. behind the Front Line; (3) the Subsidiary Line or 2nd Support Line, about 1,000 yards behind the Front Line. This sub-line, as it was called, was the rest line where troops generally interchanged after about four days in the Front Line. The communicating trenches running up to the front from the sub-line in the rear were called avenues or streets and were named after famous streets, etc., in Great Britain, Canada, etc., all according to the troops who made the trenches in the early part of the War.

This was the Battalion's first experience at holding the line, and one or two "straffs" on our part and the enemy reply, taught the men to keep their heads down, and early experience mentions that under the Fire step was a safe place. However, there was no great activity to recall any excitement in this Sector.

After holding there for ten days we were relieved at night and marched to rest billets near SAILLY for four days and were transferred from the 14th to the 15th Brigade. Our rest was spent in supplying working parties to the front and support lines.

On the 24th September we again went in to garrison the front line, this time in the LEVANTE Sector, near the site of a village called PETILION. Here we had a "Company Sector" in both front and support line and were attached to the 60th Batt., A.I.F., under Lieut.Col. Duigan. Battalion Headquarters were at Rifle House, about 800 yards in the rear of front line. The communication trench to the front line in this Sector was called V. C. Sap, after that gallant Irishman, Sergt. O'Grady, who won his V.C. at that particular spot. This was a much livelier Sector, frequently shelled, and *minenwerfers* were often sent over; we, in return, practised on the enemy with trench mortars, grenades, etc. It was here that we lost the first killed of our Battalion by enemy action, Corp. F. S. Des Barres (Opotiki) on the 30th September.

Leave to the United Kingdom was now opened, and the Battalion received a small allotment of three per week. The Adjutant, Lieut. McLennan, A.I.F., was the first to go, and his place was taken temporarily by 2nd Lieut. G. Clark Walker (No. 1 Company).

Transport lines were at BAC ST. MAUR, where our cycles were also stored, they being useless in trench warfare.

It was the Battalion's privilege to furnish a guard for the Corps Commander (Lieut.-Gen. Sir A. J. Godley). This guard had so far been drawn from No. 3 Aust. Company.

On the 27th September, 1916, a change was ordered and 1 officer (2nd Lieut. J. T. Steven) and 42 other ranks from No. 1 Company were sent for a tour of duty to BAILLEUL, then the site of the Corps Headquarters.

2nd Lieut. R. W. Kebbell was admitted to hospital on the 8th October, 1916, and did not again rejoin, being sent to N.Z. sick.

On the 13th October, 1916, the 5th Australian Division was relieved by the N.Z. Division, which had just returned from its glorious battles in the SOMME, and we being attached to the 5th Division, participated in the relief and marched out, going into billets in RUE de FIEFS. The 5th A.I.F. Division moved away south and we were attached to the 1st N.Z. Infantry Brigade (Brig.-Gen. Johnson) for tactical purposes. The Adjutant (Lieut. McLennan) having returned from leave resumed his duties.

On 15th October, 2nd Lieut. G. Clark Walker went to 2nd Army Central School of Instruction at WISQUES for a month's course in general duties.

Congratulatory and appreciative letters relative to our work in the line were received from the Corps Commander through G.O.C. 5th Division and from the C.O. 60th A.I.F. Battalion.

14/10/16.

MAJOR H. E. EVANS,
  C.O. 2nd Anzac, C.C. Bn.

DEAR MAJOR,

I wish to place on record my appreciation of your Unit's excellent work during the period of our joint occupation of the PETILION trenches. Your own activity and enthusiasm were reflected in every member of your Unit, and your Battalion left an excellent record of work and discipline to their credit. I wish you and your Officers and men the best of good luck at all times. We shall be thinking of you on our Somme tour.

    Sincerely yours,
     (Sd.) J. DUIGAN, Lieut.-Col.
         C.O. 60th Bn.,
         A.I.F.

R. S. M. Hay was promoted to 2nd Lieut., 2nd October, 1916.

After the Battalion had been in rest billets for two days, orders were received to move into new billets at BAC ST. MAUR, where we were directly under the N.Z. Division, and the men were employed as working parties in the R.E. yard.

Captain H. D. McHugh and 9 other ranks were sent to the N.Z. Reinforcement Camp near SAILLY, Captain McHugh to be Officer Commanding Reinforcement details. 2nd Lieut. C. A. Dickeson, N.Z. (R) B. joined the Battalion on transfer, 23rd October, 1916.

On the 29th October, 1916, the Unit was transferred to Frank's Force, a composite Division composed of a Brigade each, N.Z. (2nd Brigade) and 103rd Brigade (Imperial Infantry), and engaged in holding the line from HOUPLINES to BOIS GRENIER. The Battalion marched (without cycles) *via* Erquinghem to Armentieres on the afternoon of the 30th October, where it occupied billets in RUE SADI CARNOT. Next day it moved up to the line and joined the 25th Battalion Northumberland Fusiliers (Lieut.-Col. Stewart) being attached to that Battalion for tactical purposes. Rear Headquarters and Transport were located in BOULEVARD FAUDHERBE in ARMENTIERES.

We took over a Company Sector in the line having two of our Companies in the front line and the third in the Subsidiary line. Advanced Headquarters at Square Farm (Chapelle Armentieres). We remained in this Sector for four weeks, changing from front to S. S. line every four days.

The Battalion organised a raid on enemy positions to take place on the night of the 18th November. The party consisted of 2nd Lieut. J. G. Jamieson (Aus. Coy.) and 15 other ranks drawn from all companies. The party was withdrawn from the line and underwent considerable training. The raid was not successful, owing to a heavy enemy barrage preventing the raiding

The Adjutant and his Staff.

R.Q.M.S. and Staff.

party from reaching its objective. A small reinforcement draft of 2nd Lieut. Garden, R.L., and 30 other ranks arrived on the 16th November.

Frank's Force was relieved by the 3rd Australian Division on the 27th November, 1916. Our tour of duty being completed, we were relieved and marched out on the 27th November. Cycles were re-issued at Bac St. Maur and the Unit cycled to Doulieu where billets were arranged.

Our casualties while attached to Frank's Force were as follows :—

        Killed   Private A. F. George
                    ,,   T. P. Milne
             and 12 wounded.

Brig.-Gen. Trevor, G.O.C. 103rd Infantry Brigade (34th 1 Division) sent a congratulatory letter to our C.O. and thanked the Unit for its assistance and commended it for its soldierly qualities.

Chapter VI.

TRAINING—WITH THE CAVALRY.

Our new billets were situated about one mile from DOULIEU and as we were to stay there for the winter months, the Corps let us have some huts and other material to make ourselves comfortable. Training in various subjects was carried on every day. Sports were indulged in, and leave being opened to England a number of men got away for the usual ten days. The weather gradually got colder and the hard frosts started. The cold was severe on us, coming as we did from sunny climes. The Platoon from No. 2 Company under Lieut. Comer, who had been with the N.Z. Division to the Somme and had been through all the adventures of the Division, returned to the Battalion on 6th December. The G.S.O. I. (Major Temperley) of the Division sent a letter to the C.O. conveying the G.O.C. Division's appreciation of the excellent work done by this Platoon.

Christmas was celebrated by an extra special dinner being put on, officers messing with the men on this occasion. A splendid menu was arranged by the Company cooks, whose health was loudly toasted at the conclusion of the meal. Our dear folk in New Zealand were not forgotten, as the toast of "New Zealand, Home and Beauty" was the brightest and best of the day, and why not, for most of the cheer that adorned our tables came from far-away New Zealand.

Instructional Schools, under the auspices of Army and Corps, embracing General Courses, Bombing, Bayonet Fighting, Sniping, Gas, Musketry, Signalling, etc., were in full swing during the winter months, and this Battalion sent several Officers and N.C.O.'s for instruction, with the result that considerable benefit was derived. Early in January, 1917, it was decided to equip Cyclist Battalions with Lewis Guns on the scale of two guns per Company (six in Battalion) and Officers and men were instructed to proceed to the G. H. Q. Lewis Gun School at LE TOUQUET, near Etaples, for instruction.

Training was continued during January when the weather permitted, and in addition the Officers and N.C.O.'s carried out a reconnaissance of the whole Corps front, in order to become familiar with roads and tracks, positions of Brigade and Brigade Headquarters, front line, etc., in view of offensive operations to take place later on.

On 15th February the Corps Mounted Regt. left for attachment to 2nd Cavalry Division near BOULOGNE for training. Major C. H. Evans proceeded on leave to United Kingdom for a period of ten days, Captain H. McHugh commanding the Battalion (temporarily) in his absence.

On the 1st January, 1917, orders were received for the Battalion to proceed by route march to HENNEV-EUX, near BOULOGNE, there to rejoin the Corps Mounted Regiment and be attached to 2nd Cavalry Division for combined training in open warfare. Accordingly the necessary orders were issued by Battalion Headquarters, and at 9 a.m., 2nd February, the Battalion set out in full marching order with transport. The distance, some 50 miles or so, had to be done in two days. The route selected was from Daulieu via RUE-PRO-VOST, NEUF BERQUIN, MERVILLE, LESART, HAVERSKERQUE, THIENNES-AIRE, THEROU-ANNE-DOHEM, REMILLY, WAVRANS to LUMBRES, where the Battalion billeted for the night. The day was intensely cold and the roads frozen, and in some places covered with snow so deep as to render riding impossible, and the task of pushing a loaded cycle up hill through snow was a hard one, especially after leaving THEROUANNE, as the country was very hilly.

Arriving at LUMBRES we found billets all arranged and allotted by Lieut. G. Clark Walker (the Battalion

Billetting Officer) who was in charge of the advance party. It was a very cold night and no heating conveniences existed in the staging billets, but the majority of the men were provided with beds by the inhabitants of that town who did everything possible to make the men comfortable. LUMBRES will be remembered by many for the hospitality extended on that cold night. The distance covered that day was roughly thirty miles. Next morning at 9 a.m. the Battalion moved *en route* again towards their final destination. This time we kept to the main road "ROUTE NATIONAL" STOMER BOULOGNE Road. These National roads of France are well built and substantial, but as they are mostly very straight, the builders were not particular as to gradients. Some of our climbs were long and steep and our energy and endurance was severely taxed in negotiating some of the rises, particularly on a frozen road which was as slippery as glass. Spills were frequent and our temper sullen.

We arrived at HENNEVEUX about 1 p.m. after a ride of about thirteen miles. Our advance party had secured us good billets in farms which were made very comfortable. Battalion Headquarters was in a fine Chateau owned by the Countess de Belleville. In the next village, BOURNENVILLE, the Otago Mounted Rifles were located, with the other squadrons at CREMAREST and BELLEBRUN ; the Motor M.G. Battery at ALINETHUN ; Regimental Headquarters in a Chateau about a mile from our location. The whole of Corps Mounted Troops were attached to the 9th Cavalry Brigade under Brig. Gen. Leggard, D.S.O., for training.

For the first week little outdoor work was done as the weather was very wintry and snow fell frequently. Training consisted in Lectures on Compass Map Reading, etc. As soon as the weather was suitable, manœuvres were carried out daily, such as Advance and Flank Guards, Outposts, etc., and much valuable instruction gained. We covered long distances on cycles, and the training was thoroughly enjoyed by all ranks. We were only ten miles from BOULOGNE and leave was given to half the Unit every Sunday for the day and this made a good break in the work.

DESVRES, a large manufacturing town celebrated for its pottery, was about six miles distant as well as other small places of interest.

Our period of training ended on the 13th March, when orders were received to return to our Corps Area. On 15th March the Battalion marched out. Our route was *via* LUMBRES ARQUES to RACQUINGHEM where we billetted for the night. The weather was much warmer and the roads free from frost, consequently progress was easier. Next morning we departed at 9 a.m. and returned to Doulieu *via* Aire Haverskerque and Merville. On arrival we reoccupied the same billets that we vacated some six weeks beforehand. Our transport (2nd Lieut. Hay in charge) did not travel with us either going to Henneveux or returning. It took three days each way.

Chapter VII.

CABLE LAYING.

On return to our permanent area, training was carried on and the lessons learnt with the Cavalry were adopted in our manœuvres.

To provide protection of ammunition dumps against enemy bombing aircraft, a detachment of the Battalion Lewis guns—6 with gun teams complete—were sent to STEENBECQUE where there were several large army dumps of big gun ammunition. Lieuts. G. L. Comer and G. Clark Walker and 48 other ranks were employed on this work under direction of an Anti-Aircraft Battery.

During March the officers of the Battalion reconnoitred the whole of the Corps front with a view of becoming acquainted with it in the event of operations. Twelve selected men were sent to the Corps Headquarters for training as Corps Guides. These men learned every road, trench and sap in the area and were most useful to new troops arriving.

A small detachment under 2nd Lieut. A. C. P. Hay was sent to the vicinity of OUTERSTEENE to fell some 100 huge trees for sawmilling purposes. The expert axemen, including Private J. E. Shewry (the N.Z. Champion, 1916), soon made short work of the job and the work was well done too.

On the 1st April the Unit was ordered to proceed to REGINA Camp near PLOEGSTEERT and to be attached to the N.Z. Working Battalion under Major Pow, N.Z. (R) B. for work on Cable Burying under A. D. Signals 2nd Anzac Corps. The work we were engaged on was called "The Corps Buried System of Communications" and consisted of burying cable containing telephone wires in a trench 6, 7 and 8 feet deep (according to the proximity of the front line) in order the better to preserve the lines from damage by

Aero Photo of Messines

Dotted line in black denotes course of track made by the N.Z. Cyclists on the morning of the Battle, 7/16/17.

enemy shell fire. All this work was carried out behind the front line in the area which received the full benefit of the enemy's wrath. The ground through which we dug was in many cases a sea of shell holes. Naturally the ground was very loose, and I have in many cases seen where a digger would be just completing his task (7 x 6 x 2½ feet) and have the whole trench fall in. The supervising officer was responsible for burying 7 feet and the trench would have to be redug. This was very disheartening to the men, especially when digging at night—a case then of feeling your way ("'no lights allowed.'")

The N.Z. Working Battalion had been in existence for about three weeks and had buried some 10,000 yards or so. The whole system of connecting the front, reserve and support lines, batteries, various Headquarters, entailed the digging of some 23 miles of running trench.

On the 3rd April Major Pow rejoined his Battalion and the command of the Working Battalion was given to Major C. H. Evans, who continued the programme until the job was completed on 19th May. As the lines in the back areas were completed by day, the work in the forward areas had to be done by night as the ground was under direct enemy observation from MESSINES. The personnel of the Working Battalion frequently changed, Brigades withdrew Companies and substituted others. During the period there were attached Australian Light Horse and O.M.R. from the 2nd Anzac Mounted Regiment and a Company from the 3rd Australian Division, besides our Battalion and the three N.Z. Division Companies. The whole work comprised over 23 miles of trench, and the wires buried averaged 50 pairs (one line had 84 pairs) sufficient to make one line with return wire of 1,100 miles.

The value of the system was manifested in later operations when it enabled communications to be kept intact despite the heaviest shelling.

On the 19th May the system was completed and the Working Battalion disbanded, the various Units returning to their Brigades, etc. The Corps Commander sent a very appreciative letter to the troops and thanked them for their good work. All ranks worked hard, despite unfavourable conditions, oftentimes in water and mud to the waist, heavy shelling, etc. Our Battalion finished its work with the Working Battalion on the 15th May and moved into new billets near STEEN-WERK, where training was continued.

It may be interesting to mention in regard to the cable burying operations the Battalion was engaged in during the years 1917-1918 that the total length of trench, excavated to a depth of 7 feet and over, by and under the supervision of the Battalion was over 56 miles, and as the average number of wires laid was over 50 pairs, the total length of wire works out at about 5,600 miles.

Chapter VIII.

BATTLE OF MESSINES.

Preparations for an advance on our particular Army front were obvious, although little was communicated to us by the Higher Command. Guns and ammunition of all calibre began to arrive. Troops and many other signs, including the vastly increased traffic on the roads, could only mean one thing, and all ranks were keenly interested as to their part in the job. To control the traffic the greater portion of two Companies was sent out on point duty to control and direct the endless streams of waggons, lorries, cars, troops, etc. Captain A. H. Richards was in charge of one area for traffic and Lieut. Lord, A.I.F., another.

During the latter part of May, 1917, matters in regard to the projected attack on the enemy positions on our Army front, assumed definite shape. The Army front at that time embraced that sector of country just south of Hill 60 (S.E. of YPRES) to Lys River. Our Corps which was acting on front WYTCHAETE to the River Lys issued orders administrative and tactical and assigned each Unit its part in the show.

The Corps Mounted Troops consisting of the 2nd Anzac Corps Mounted Regiment, 2nd Anzac Corps Cyclist Battalion and the 7th Motor M.G. Battery were allotted the following tasks :—

1. M.M.G. Battery to be detached and come under orders of G.M.G.O. for employment in the M.G. Barrage.
2. Mounted Regiment to move forward three hours after zero hour and engage enemy in front of Infantry, capture guns and obtain information, etc.
3. Cyclist Battalion to prepare a track from our Reserve line, through our support and front

line system, across No Man's Land, and through German trenches to a point called MIDDLEFARM about 500 yards north of MESSINES, so as to enable the Mounted Men to get through, as otherwise it was impossible for the horses to move through the tangle of wire and trenches and shell holes.

The reconnaissance of the line was made by the C.O. Mounted Troops (Lieut.-Col. Hindhaugh), Major R. B. Wood 2nd i/c Mounted Troops, Major Evans and Captain McHugh (Cyclists).

The portion of the track in rear of our own front line was prepared beforehand and marked out with pickets. The work of making this portion was entrusted to Capt. McHugh (O.C. No. 1 Coy.) who with his party carried out the work in two nights. This work entailed the filling in of shell holes, cutting through our own wire and bridging over one stream and four communication trenches, besides having all material carried to the front line trenches which was required forward on the morning of the battle. The work forward of our trenches could not be reconnoitred, but the ground was carefully studied from the front line.

The attack was fixed for the 7th June, 1917, and the zero hour, 3.10 a.m. The details of our work were thought out and definite jobs were told off to certain parties. There were some 1,800 yards to do, and as time was short, careful organisation was necessary to ensure completion.

The following Officers, etc., were engaged :—

Major Evans, to reconnoitre and peg off the line to be followed by.

No. 1 Party, to clear wire and mark line. 2nd Lieut. W. L. C. McLean and 13 men.

No. 2 Party. To clear timber and remove obstacles. 2nd Lieut. A. C. P. Hay and 30 men.

No. 3 Party. To fill shell holes, trenches, and level the ground. Lieut. Griffiths (A.I.F.) and 84 men.

Battle of Messines

No. 4 Party. To bridge streams. Captain McHugh and 25 men.

Balance of Unit in Reserve in old front line to carry on track further if required and to replace casualties. Battalion Headquarters and F.A. Dressing Station in old front line.

On the morning of 7th June, at 2 15 a.m., the parties left their billets near STEENWERCK and cycled to WHITE GATES on Hill 63, a distance of 7 or 8 miles. On the way up, when near ROMARIN, enemy gas was encountered and gas masks had to be put on. Further on, higher ground was reached, where the gas was less oppressive. On reaching our rendezvous everything was dead still, not a gun had been heard for an hour or so, when suddenly a huge 12in. gun in the rear was fired, at which signal 19 mines along the whole army front were exploded ; thus at 3.10, zero hour, the Battle of Messines was heralded.

As we were not due at our front line till zero hour plus one hour, we had plenty of time to work our way up to our objective (the front line). On arrival, the front line was being "straffed" heavily, and there our casualties started. Private A. Duff was killed outright and several men wounded. Punctually to time all parties arrived and the work was started and the whole track finished about half-an-hour less time than was allotted us. Every man worked hard, despite the fact that the enemy shelling was intense and several casualties occurred. In bridging the Steenbecque Stream the locality was subjected to very heavy shell fire. Private Cairns was killed outright, and Privates C. L. Anstey and C. Barwick subsequently dying of wounds received in this area, besides 19 men wounded.

At 7.30 prompt the Mounted men appeared in view and moving at a smart trot along the winding track we had made. Their advent cheered the men, both wounded and sound. The Irish Infantry on our left gave them a cheer as they passed over the hill. They too suffered several casualties, but did their job well and earned abundant praise for the valuable information gained.

Our men, their job finished, remained on Messines Ridge in reserve, ready to carry on if required. At 2 p.m. they were withdrawn, and picking up our reserve troops at BOYLE'S FARM on the Wulverghem-Messines Road, we withdrew to the top of Hill 63 and bivouacked. Next morning, in anticipation of having to move forward again, two reconnoitring patrols were sent out to ascertain condition of roads to MESSINES. 2nd Lieut. DICKESON, C.A., and 2nd Lieut. Griffiths, V., were in charge, and these parties had a lively time getting through the enemy's retaliatory barrage.

The Battle meanwhile had gone well, and all objectives gained. The attacking troops were the 3rd Australian Division (right), N.Z. Division (centre) and the Irish on the left. Our part, though not spectacular, was important, in fact just as important as any other, and earned the highest praise of the Corps Commander. On the whole Army front each Corps Troops was allotted the same task as ours, but was not so successful as we were. One Corps got its cavalry out at 3 p.m. in the afternoon ; the other, not at all. The behaviour of our men was splendid. To advance against an enemy during a heavy fire, when there is a chance of hitting back, is quite a different matter from working under heavy fire where no such chance exists.

The following decorations were awarded :—
D.S.O.   Major C. Hellier Evans
M.C.'   Capt. H. D. McHugh
M.M.   Sergt. A. H. Coe
          Sergt. A. C. Anderson
          Sergt. R. H. Sly
          Private R. J. Ringham
          Private F. J. Sharpe

On the 11th instant the Mounted Troops were ordered up to Hyde Park Corner (Ploegsteert Wood) to assist the 3rd Australian Division on some minor tactical operation. At 8 p.m. we arrived at Ploegsteert Wood and received orders to take up a position east of Ploegsteert Wood by night, with a view of attacking and taking the Sugar Refinery in the early morning. This was modified by later orders and our task was to establish a line of outposts near Thatched Cottage. These two parties, about 30 strong, with Lewis guns, set out after dark directed by guides whose knowledge of the country was very *vague*. One party got lost and returned ; the other under Lt. Lord (Aust. Coy.) succeeded in reaching its objective at 2.a.m. Battalion Headquarters and also those of the Mounted Regiments were established in BUNHILL Row, a strong breastwork running through the wood. The enemy shelled the Wood all night and it wasn't very comfortable. Next day nothing happened and *at dusk* our outposts were withdrawn and the Unit then returned to permanent billets at Steenwerck without having suffered any casualties.

Next day, 13th June, orders were issued to the Unit to continue cable burying from our old front line to points forward in the recaptured territory. A reconnaissance of the work was made by the officers who decided that owing to visibility it was advisable to work by night instead of by day. Work on the job was started that night and continued for three weeks, when it was completed. About 5 miles of trench were dug in this job. The cable burying parties were frequently subjected to enemy fire and casualties occurred. Sergt. R. H. Sly and Corp. Bellamy were conspicuous in their behaviour in getting the wounded away one night when we were caught in heavy shell fire. Both these N.C.O.'s were wounded, and despite the heavy fire, carried the others to safety, returning for those left behind. For their conspicuous bravery, Sergt. Sly was awarded a Bar to his M.M., and Corp. Bellamy awarded the M.M. Privates A. P. Kay and M. A. Pankhurst were killed in this area on the 10th July.

On the 26th June, H.R.H. the Duke of Connaught visited the front and inspected representatives from all the Corps Units at BAILLEUL. Our Battalion was represented by several Officers and N.C.O.'s.

On the 6th July the Corps Commander inspected all the Corps Mounted Troops at our billets, and presented ribands of the decorations awarded for the Messines Battle.

CONCERT CELEBRATING FIRST ANNIVERSARY OF THE BATTALION, 1917.

FIRST ANNIVERSARY DINNER, 1917.

Chapter IX.

THE FIRST ANNIVERSARY OF THE BATTALION.

On the 21st July, the first anniversary of the formation of the Battalion was held, and to celebrate this occasion sports were held in which items were included for the Mounted Regiment. All ranks thoroughly enjoyed the day, which was free from work. Furthermore, a dinner for all ranks was specially prepared by our cooks and the usual ration, augmented by extras, provided an excellent meal. A concert was held after dinner and the Battalion was photographed.

The Corps Commander, desiring to reward men whose services had been valuable, but who by reason of their employment in the Unit were debarred from winning distinction in the line, instituted an admirable system of presenting Parchment Certificates called "Record of Good Service." On recommendation, these certificates were granted in limited number. The following were recommended in the Battalion and received the award :—

2nd Lieut.	C. G. Johnson	Quartermaster
L. Corpl.	J. S. Hill	Artificer
Driver	A. Grant	Headquarters
Private	W. Attneave	Storeman No. 3 Coy.
Private	R. C. Cruse	Cook No. 3 Coy.

During August the Battalion was employed in various ways, cable burying, traffic control, training ; several officers and men being sent to special courses.

Towards the end of August the Corps, which had been continually in the southern sector of the 2nd Army front, was withdrawn, and sent out to back areas for a rest, this Battalion moving on the 2nd September to LA MOTTE area and going into billets near VIEUX BERQUIN. The Battalion Lewis Guns and teams were sent to Hazebrouck on anti-aircraft defence of the railway station. The Mounted Regiment moved out of the Cavalry Area near BOULOGNE for training on the 7th.

We were just beginning to settle down when orders were received to report to X Corps in DICKEBUSCH area for employment under A. D. Signals on our old job of burying cable. Accordingly we moved on the 8th September by route march to LA CLYTTE where we were billetted. Our job was to assist this Corps (X) to complete its buried system. They already had two Battalions of the N.Z. (R) B. working for them, but their system was incomplete, and some "linking up" was required.

Our route was about a mile through SANCTUARY WOOD, the scene of some bloody battles in 1915, where the Canadians fought so gallantly and where the enemy first used poison gas. The work was by night, and our first night on this job we were shelled lavishly with Mustard Gas, from which some 50 odd men and 1 officer went to hospital next day from gas burns on their bodies.

We finished our work with the X Corps on the 17th September, and received orders to move back to our Corps Area. On the 19th we moved out of La Clytte with our destination as RENESCURE *via* BAILLEUL STAPLE, but on arrival there were told to go on to ARQUES where we halted for the night. The distance travelled was 32 miles, mostly against wind, much traffic, and its attendant dust.

Next morning we left ARQUES at 9 a.m. and made BOUVELINGHEM (15 miles) by noon, and there settled down in fairly good billets.

We thought that we would be in this area for at least a fortnight, but were hardly settled down when the Corps which had been training and resting in the area were ordered once more into the fray and we had to return with them. So after three days' rest we took the

FIRST ANNIVERSARY OF THE BATTALION

road again and made some farm houses near CASSEL that night ; next day on to WATOU, thence to billets near POPERINGHE.

Next day it was ascertained that we were to be used on our old job of cable burying east of YPRES to complete the system required for the forthcoming assault on PASSCHENDAELE RIDGES.

The new badge for the N.Z. Companies was approved and issued in August, 1917, It was a similar badge to that worn by Imperial Cyclist Units, having a wheel with crossed rifles surmounted by a crown and a scroll underneath with the words N.Z. Cyclist Corps (see illustration). also shoulder badges, bearing the letters N.Z.C.C. were issued to the N.Z. personnel.

The following letter was received from the G.O.C. X Corps :—

X Corps, No. 852.

HEADQUARTERS,
    2ND ANZAC.

It is difficult for me adequately to express to you my gratitude for the splendid work of the 1st, 2nd, 3rd and 4th Battalions, 3rd New Zealand (Rifle) Brigade and the 11 Anzac Corps Cyclists in burying cable on my Corps front during the last three weeks. Their achievement in digging over 13,000 yards of cable trench, laying the cable, and banking it up from three to four feet is an extraordinary one ; the keenness that they displayed is universally admired, and their skill is acknowledged to be an example to any troops. Will you please tell these gallant men how much, while I deplore the casualties they suffered, I appreciate both their valuable work and their soldierly spirit.

        (sd.)   K. W. MORELAND,
                Lieut.-General,
           Commanding Xth Corps.

H. Q. Xth Corps,
    10th September, 1917.

CHAPTER X.

GRAVENSTRAFEL—PASSCHENDAELE.

Our work in this sector was not to dig trenches, but by our practical knowledge of cable work, we acted as Signal Engineer personnel, having complete charge of the running out of the cable, laying it, and in generally supervising the work. The actual digging was done by the first and 3rd Battalions N.Z.R.B. The Unit moved up to BRANDHOEK into Camp there. Major Evans, D.S.O., was given charge of the whole work, and with Lieut. Dickeson in charge of cable, moved forward to GOLDFISH CHATEAU where Headquarters were established. The system consisted of about 11 miles of trench in two main forward lines linked at three places by lateral lines.

The whole work was divided into two parts, Major Evans taking the Southern line with Lieut. Lord and No. 3 Australian Company (cable) and the 3rd Battalion N.Z.R.B. (diggers), Captain McHugh, M.C., taking the northern line with Captain A. H. Richards and No. 1 and 2 N.Z. Companies (cable) and the 1st Battalion N.Z.R.B. as diggers.

Work was started on the evening of the 27th September on both routes and was continued for ten nights (not continuous) until finished. The Riflemen, under the capable guidance of their Officers and N.C.O.'s worked remarkably well, and for 800 men to accomplish the average length of close on a mile a night was a wonderful achievement.

The Passchendaele advance started on the 4th October, and by that time both lines were almost up to the "hopping off" place. From that forward the work proceeded on the heels of the advancing troops. The enemy shelling throughout was heavy and the going bad

GRAVENSTRAFEL—PASSCHENDAELE 49

owing to the rain and the sea of shell holes filled with water, but the men stuck to their work well and accomplished a result which any army may be proud of.

The technical work of handling the cable, which included transportation over difficult ground, the reeling out of cable, laying, and marking trench, was done entirely by this unit. Its officers supervised the whole work, and no difficulty or obstacle was allowed to hinder them in their desire to complete a satisfactory job. Lieut. C. A. Dickeson was in charge of the cable and responsible for getting it to the end of the roads in the sector, and in spite of many difficulties, owing to the awful weather and lack of roads, never once failed. For this work, under the difficult conditions existing, this Officer was awarded the M.C.

Latterly, when the N.Z.R.B. was withdrawn from the work to take its place in the fighting, parties from the 1st and 2nd Brigades were detailed to carry on, and with their help the whole system was finally finished, and on the 17th October the Canadian Corps took over our Corps front, and we, with the rest of the troops, left BRANDHOEK and moved to a place near Steenvoorde for the night. Next day we proceeded to Hazebrouck and went into billets there for reorganisation and rest. We stayed there a week, and on the 26th received orders to proceed to FRUGES area.

Next morning at 9 a.m. we marched out and made a small village called FIEFS, a distance of 25 miles. Our route lay through STEENBECQUE, AIRE, ST. HILARE, WESTREHEM, At Fiefs the Battalion was billetted in the CHATEAU BEAUCNINE, once a beautiful place, but now much spoiled by war's destruction.

Next day our march was continued, and early in the afternoon we reached AMBRICOURT, a small village which had not previously had British troops billetted there. It was in this village that some of the peasants chased their pigs out of the stye for the men to sleep in.

Only a little of that treatment is sufficient, and it did not take many minutes to convince the people they were dealing with soldiers ; after that the billets were fairly good.

This village is quite close to the famous old-time battlefield of AGINCOURT, where King Henry V. of England defeated the French in 1415.

We stayed in this area for about two weeks and enjoyed the rest, and carried on useful training, the country there being very suitable for field training.

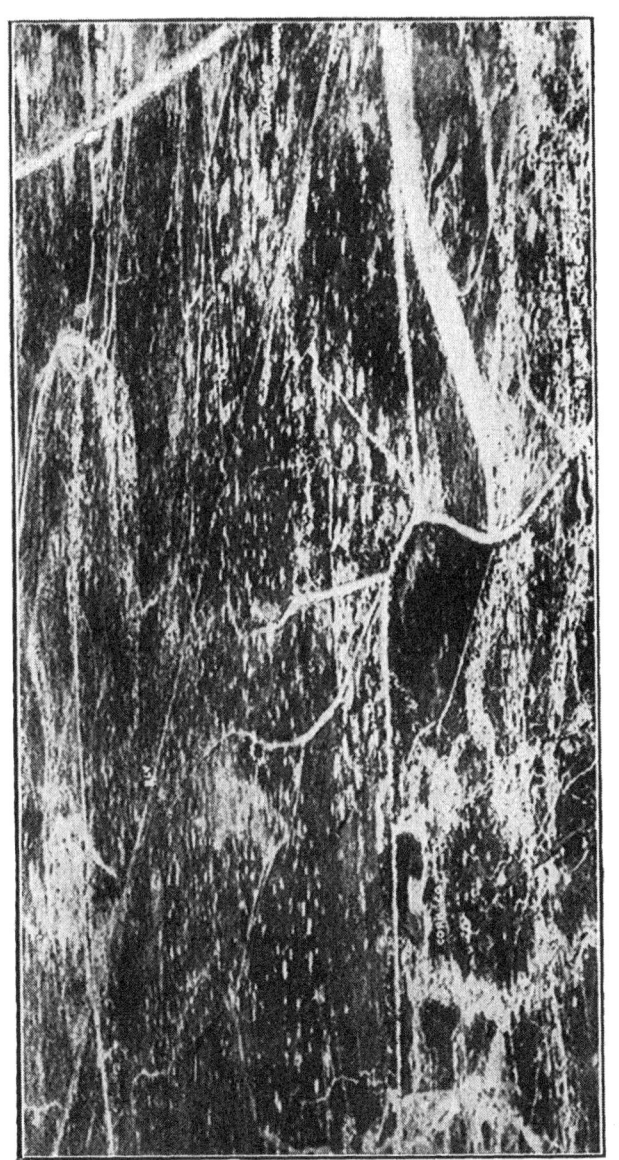

AREO PHOTO OF THE FAMOUS YPRES SECTOR.

Chapter XI.

YPRES.

On the 13th November we marched out to rejoin our Corps which had its Headquarters at ABEELE in Belgium. Our first destination was MERCK ST. LEVIEN, near FAUQUEMBERQUES, next day on to ZUYTPEENE near CASSEL, and next day through Poperinghe to a place called VANCOUVER CAMP near VLAMERTINGHE. This camp consisted of wood and iron huts which had been built in 1915 and were in an indifferent state of repair. However we soon made them comfortable, and also erected earth walls round each hut three feet above floor level for protection against lateral bursting bombs from aircraft.

We soon learned that our job was to be cable laying and the system embraced several forward lines in the newly captured territory east of YPRES. Approximately some 22 miles of trench would be required. As before, we were to supply the technical personnel, the diggers being supplied by a Battalion from the 2nd N.Z. Infantry Brigade.

On 17th November a party of Officers and N.C.O.'s proceeded to survey the routes. The party consisted of Major Evans, Captains McHugh and Richards, Lieut. Lord (Coy. Commanders), Lieut. J. T. Steven and others, and journeyed by motor lorry to HELLFIRE CORNER, thence on foot to Westhoek. After three hours the party was returning from the reconnaissance when the enemy started one of his 'area'' shoots, and shells fell in close proximity to the party. One shell landed just alongside the road and Lieut. Steven was hit by a fragment. He was carried to the nearest dressing station, but died before reaching it. Lieut. Steven had only returned to the Unit from hospital where he was admitted on receiving a slight wound at PASSCHEN-DAELE. He was thoroughly capable, a keen sport, and extremely popular with the men. His loss was keenly felt by all ranks. Lieut. Steven's death marked the first of the officers of the Unit to make the supreme sacrifice.

Work was started two days later ; two parties were engaged and continued almost continuously until Christmas. The enemy shelling was considerable in this area ; every day marked casualties, either our own Unit or the Battalion digging for us, sometimes both. In the first week on this work, Lieuts. Lord and Griffiths (A.I.F.) were both wounded, the latter severely, near THE BUTTE, POLYGON WOOD, and Private A. Stokes was killed a few days later.

The weather gradually became colder, and winter set in. Recreational training was not neglected and two good football teams were selected, A and B teams. Many hard games were fought out with teams from the N.Z. Division. Imperial teams were also met, but proved easy.

Our Lewis guns and teams were sent into the forward area to protect the heavy artillery from enemy aircraft, and three posts were established, one each at HOOGE, RAILWAY WOOD and WESTHOEK RIDGE. These teams were changed weekly.

Early in December the C.O., Major Evans, D.S.O., went to England on leave, Captain McHugh, M.C., taking over command during his absence.

Christmas arrived and was celebrated as usual with cheer provided by our good people in New Zealand.

On 1st January, 1918, the old 2nd Anzac Corps was renamed XXII. Corps, and we became the "XXII. Corps Cyclist Battalion."

Early in January Lieut. A. C. P. Hay and Corps. McKenzie and Agnew left for England. They had been selected for some special secret service abroad, no one knew what for or where to. It has since transpired that they went east (Mesopotamia).

The Australian Company (No. 3 Coy.) were withdrawn from the Battalion on the 16th January and left to join the Australian Corps Cyclist Battalion. At the time of parting it is shown how we regretted their leaving us and what firm friends we had made. Although at times minor differences occurred, they were all good fellows, and during the eighteen months they formed part of the Battalion, they did their "bit" to uphold the traditions of the service.

To bring the Battalion up to full strength again authority was given by G.O.C., N.Z.E.F., for the formation of another N.Z. Company. Accordingly applications for transfer were invited from the Division; the Officers and Senior N.C.O.'s were to be found by promotion within the Battalion.

The following appointments were made in the new Company which was designated "No. 3 Company."

Company Commander	Lieut. G. L. Comer
C.S.M.	C.S.M. T. H. Dickinson
Sergeants	Sergt. R. H. Sly, M.M.
	and Sergt. T. C. Hodgson

Additional officers were to be selected by G.O.C. in London from reinforcements and sent on to complete.

Parchment Certificates, Record of Good Service, were awarded by the Corps Commander for period 15th January to 1st November, 1917, as under:—

Private	E. C. Cragg	Storeman
Private	W. Fitzmaurice	Driver
Private	E. J. Morris	Cook
Private	W. J. Cheshire	Cook
Corporal	R. J. Hyde	Transport Corpl.

On 24th January our camp was bombed by enemy aircraft, one hut being hit direct; Private P. Mudie and four men wounded; the former died from wounds next day.

Lieut. C. A. Dickeson, M.C., was appointed Adjutant with acting rank of Captain, *vice* Lieut. H. J. McLennan (A.I.F.) who left with the Australian Company

The selection of the personnel for the new Company from men in the Division who had volunteered for transfer was proceeded with. Preference was given to men of long service in the Division, and they were an excellent lot of men. Training into the ways of the Unit Drill, both foot and cycle, was carried out. Early in February the cable burying was resumed (this time the 3rd O.I.R. were digging) and was continued intermittently till early March. On 12th February Sergt. W. H. Thomas and Corp. Foulds were awarded the Croix de Guere (Belgian) for gallantry in the field and received their decorations from the Belgian Army Commander at Abeele.

As usual the Battalion supplied a number of men for traffic control duties in forward areas. This work was strenuous and responsible, and during March all forward road junctions received particular attention from the enemy long range guns, the post in YPRES being well "straffed." Whilst on duty there Private J. S. Clark was killed and several of our men wounded during the month.

The rest of February and part of March was spent alternately working on cable and training, with the usual recreations. Football matches were frequent. The N.Z. Divisional Theatre, and others of similar sort, were handy, and everybody found plenty to occupy any spare time on their hands.

Lieut. J. T. Steven
Killed in action at Westhoek, near Ypres, 17/11/17.

Chapter XII.

ENEMY OFFENSIVE OF MARCH, 1918.

March 21st, when the enemy started his big push, found us still working at cable laying, and many conjectures flew around as to what our next job would be. The N.Z. Division hurriedly left our area and went south, where they finally added fresh glories to their record near Albert, and we regretted their leaving our special front.

On the night of the 26th March we received orders to be ready to move at short notice, and next morning our C.O. received orders to report to 63rd Brigade, 21st Imperial Division, at Bedford House, near YPRES, and be prepared to take over a Battalion sector that night. The line was reconnoitred by Major Evans, D.S.O., Major McLeish (A.L.H.), Captain McHugh, M.C., and Captain Mitchell, M.C. (O.M.R.) that morning. The whole of Corps Mounted Troops were formed into a composite Battalion named the 22nd Corps Mounted Troops Composite Battalion.

Re-organisation was necessary to bring our formation to correspond with an ordinary Infantry Battalion, so four Companies were formed.

> A Company, comprising Nos. 1 and 2 Coy.'s Cyclists, under Capt. H. D. McHugh, M.C., with 2nd Lieuts. Coe, Dickinson and Branson.
>
> B Company, comprising No. 3 Coy.'s Cyclists, under Capt. G. L. Comer, with Lieut. McLean and 2nd Lieut. Highet.
>
> C Company, comprising D and part of B Squadrons, A.L.H., under Major R. McLeish, with Capt. Birnie, Lieut. Apps and Pearse.

D COMPANY, comprising the rest of B Squadron and O.M.R. Squadron, under Capt. Mitchell, M.C., with Capt. Pleasants, Lieuts. Biggar and Herbert.

Companies were about 150 strong.

The following were the composition of Battalion Headquarters :—

Major	C. H. Evans, D.S.O.	in command
Major	S. Armstrong, A.I.F.	2nd in command
Captain	— Fox, A.I.F.	M.O.
Captain	C. A. Dickenson, M.C.	Adjutant
Lieut.	C. G. Johnson	Quartermaster
Lieut.	G. Clark Walker	I.O. and M.G.O.
Lieut.	— Alder, A.I.F.	S.O.

The Battalion was organised in a remarkably short time, as it was late in the forenoon before the Commanders were back from their reconnaissance. The mounted squadrons, minus their horses, assembled at Vancouver Camp (our Headquarters).

The whole Battalion moved off at 6 p.m. in two trains (light railway) and arrived at the detraining point at 8 p.m., thence by route march to trenches—three or four miles—taking over from a Battalion of the 63rd Brigade. A and B Companies went into the front line outposts, C Company into support, and D Company in reserve. Battalion Headquarters were situated in a dugout near Hill 60.

The sector was known as SHREWSBURY FOREST and was part of the ground recaptured in July-Sept., 1917. by the 8th and 10th Corps.

The front line consisted of a line of organised shell holes and Pill Boxes (German concrete dugouts) at the foot of a fairly steep hill. No lateral communication trenches were in existence, and as the enemy overlooked us in daylight no movement was allowed, only in the dark. Rations had to be sent out overnight, and as the ground was nothing but a sea of shell holes and water, the going was very difficult. A back lamp from Company Headquarters was flashed at night to guide parties in the line to Headquarters. We remained in for nine nights, having a comparatively quiet time, and were relieved by the 146th Brigade. We journeyed out to Scottish Wood Camp for two days and then back again into the same sector, being finally relieved on the night of 12th-13th April. During our stay in this sector we had very few casualties, Private Potter being killed and six wounded.

At this time the awful cannonading going on just south of our sector in the direction of ARMENTIERES told us of further advances of the enemy. Things began to become anxious with us, and when on the 11th April the troops on our right withdrew their front line posts, it necessitated an alteration in our defences to protect our right flank which was "in the air." However, the enemy attack did not reach as far north as our sector.

On the afternoon of the 12th April, Captain McHugh and No. 1 Company were withdrawn from the line and ordered to proceed to Vancouver Camp where orders awaited them to proceed mounted and report to the 33rd Division at MONT BLANC, near Bailleul. That night the Battalion was relieved in the line by the 7th Leicesters (21st Division) and marched to Lambton Siding near Zillebeke Lake, where a train took them to Vancouver Camp, where orders awaited them that the Composite Battalion was disbanded and Mounted men were to get their horses at RENINGHELST, and Cyclists their cycles at Vancouver, and be ready to move at 7 a.m., 13th.

Chapter XIII.

KEMMEL AND METEREN AND STRAZEELE.

The balance of the Battalion comprising Battalion Headquarters and Nos. 2 and 3 Companies moved to BOESCHAEPE, leaving behind a great number of stores which it was impossible to move through lack of transport. From BOESCHAEPE we moved to LOCRE, and there received orders to establish a defensive line on the South Eastern slopes of MONT KEMMEL. This was done without delay, and two lines of posts manned. The rest of that day was quiet. The enemy had broken through at NEUVE EGLISE and we could see the battle raging in this vicinity.

On Sunday, the 14th, our Infantry (Imperial) began to fall back from NEUVE EGLISE and the ridge, and we "stood to" all night. We collected a lot of stragglers, and attached them to our little garrison. Next morning the enemy attacked on our right Crucifix Hill and Ravelsberg and made considerable progress.

We were, on the 16th, relieved by the 8th Corps Schools Battalion and we moved further east to Donegal Farm Sector where our men had a particularly hot time with enemy M.G. fire and surprise shelling, and frequently had to dislodge enemy patrols. Privates T. W. Burrows and V. E. Hudson were killed on outpost. Late that night we were pulled out and retired to Fairy Farm. The shelling on this hill had by this time become intense and casualties began to mount up.

The Mounted men, minus horses, had been sent up to dig in and occupy trenches in rear of our previous line and there were signs of French troops coming in to our relief.

A very brief stay at Fairy House was ours, and that same evening the two Companies, Nos. 2 and 3, moved once more to the top of KEMMEL to reinforce the

KEMMEL, METEREN AND STRAZEELE 59

Mounted men. The enemy shelling was most intense, every sort of gun and gas shell was used. We had numerous casualties. The killed were Privates W. E. J. Browne, T. J. Clinton, A. W. Hunter, T. E. Power, R. E. Harris. Died of wounds: C.S.M., T. C. Hodgson, Private L. L. Martin.

On the night of the 18th the French troops finally took over the defence of this sector and we withdrew to Fairy House once more, and after a night's rest left in the early morning for the vicinity of Brandhoek. We occupied some Nissen Bow Huts by the ammunition dumps as the only available billets to be had, as everywhere round us were troops, guns, horses, wagons, etc., who had possession of all the camps.

L/Sergt. W. T. N. Bond and Corp. W. H. Whiting were awarded the M.M. for bravery in action and devotion to duty.

Let us now follow the doings of No. 1 Company under Captain McHugh, M.C., on detachment with the 33rd Imperial Division. This Company moved out from Vancouver Camp on the night of the 12th April at 9 p.m. with orders to report to 33rd Division towards BAILLEUL. The night was particularly dark and the road one endless stream of traffic going and coming, so progress was slow. On nearing Bailleul we turned off towards ST. JAN'S CAPPEL where Divisional Headquarters were supposed to be, but on arrival found they had moved to MONT BLANC. We reported there at 2 a.m. and received orders to bivouac on the roadside for the remainder of the night and to report in the early morning to G.O.C. 192nd Brigade with Headquarters at Meteren. We moved at 6 a.m. next morning, 13th, arriving at 7 a.m. on outskirts of Meteren, which was being intensely shelled. It was decided to reach Headquarters which was on the other side, by running the gauntlet, and the Company was sent through in small parties. Luckily, this was achieved without casualties, though the margin was narrow. Captain McHugh reported to G.O.C.,

19.nd Brigade and was told to send out patrols to get information, as the position of the Brigade front was indefinite. These were sent out, and the whole line patrolled, and by 11 a.m. the definite line was marked on the map. On the right of Bailleul the N.Z. Entrenching Battalion was encountered, where it was learned that a whole platoon had been captured in the night, owing to having been left "in the air" by the troops on their right retiring in the night. At 2 p.m. Captain McHugh received orders to proceed to Strazeele and send back reports as to our and enemy positions and the Headquarters of our Battalions. On arrival at Strazeele patrols were sent out, and at 7 p.m. that evening a full report was furnished to Brigade Headquarters. Patrols were established throughout the night and valuable information obtained. The next morning the 1st Australian Division arrived and took over the sector, and the Company returned to Meteren to stand by. On 15th we were ordered to report to C.O. Queen's Own Battalion and did duty in the line until 18th when we were sent into reserve at MONT DES CATS. On 19th we received orders to rejoin our own Battalion at Brandhoek, and on the morning of the 20th at 5 a.m. set out, arriving at 9 a.m. Major Gen. Penny, G.O.C., 33rd Division, sent for Captain McHugh on the 19th inst. and congratulated him on the splendid work of the Company whose services he highly appreciated.

The Company had five wounded during their detachment, and Sergt. H. Gilchrist and the two Gallagher Brothers were awarded Military Medals for special gallant actions.

CHAPTER XIV.

VEIRSTRATT.

The Battalion remained in the area of Brandhoek for three days, when the enemy got our range with his guns, and as there were acres of shells (reserve dumps) around the vicinity, it was thought advisable to move. So tents were procured and the Battalion moved to an open field 1,000 yards south of POPERINGHE where a camp was erected.

At this time the battle was raging furiously. The enemy attempt to advance was being met gallantly by the French and our 21st Division, but numbers told, and the enemy was gradually making progress along the line KEMMEL-ZILLEBEKE LAKE. Things were becoming serious for the safety of the POPERINGHE FLAT, and our Unit was told to be ready to move at short notice.

On the morning of the 25th we received orders to move forward, and after reporting at Ouderdom received orders to "stop a gap" near VEIRSTRATT. We accordingly moved off (with the Mounted men) and reached Hallebast Corner amid awful shelling. We proceeded in small parties and on arrival at SWAN AND EDGAR CORNER, three enemy planes followed and peppered us with their M.G.'s. It was decided by Captain McHugh to leave the cycles on Veirstratt Road and proceed on foot in artillery formation. We were advised by a returning wounded officer that the enemy had advanced in huge numbers. Our patrols soon reported this fact, and it was impossible to get within 600 yards of the line given us to take up, owing to the enemy having advanced in such numbers it was beyond our power to push him back. The Companies took up a defensive line astride the Veirstratt Road, filling a gap of 1,000 yards, and for four days held the enemy off with determination and with such success that he did not advance past the point where our men stopped him. That night small organised out-flanking movements gained us prisoners, from whom valuable information was obtained.

Battalion Headquarters were established at Hallebast Corner, but owing to its unhealthy region for shelling moved 100 yards back next day.

On the morning of 26th April an attempt was made by Nos. 1 and 3 Companies to straighten out the line. These two Companies advanced at 5 a.m., but owing to the troops on the right flank not conforming to the action as arranged, we were left "in the air" and had to return to our original line suffering some casualties during the movement.

The C.O., Major Evans and Captain Dickeson (Adjutant) left Headquarters later in the morning to make a reconnaissance of the line. On the road down an enemy shell burst between them, killing the Adjutant instantly. Major Evans escaped unhurt, but was severely shaken by the explosion, together with having been gassed at Kemmel, and was advised by the M.O. to give in and he left for hospital that day, Captain H. D. McHugh, M.C., assuming command of the Battalion in his absence. Lieut. G. Clark Walker was appointed Adjutant.

Up to the 28th instant the Battalion held on to their positions. The enemy made no further progress, although he made several attempts which were held off by our troops. On the evening of the 28th we were relieved, and moved into support slightly right of our original line. This position was open and swampy. The men dug in during the night and remained in these slit trenches for the next two days. During the daytime no movement was allowed, so the inevitable was to remain up to the knees in water, wishing for the night to speedily come so that cramped limbs could be revived. Our cycles were still on Veirstratt Road, and received a fair amount of shellfire and were badly damaged. On the nights of 29th and 30th small parties of men who could be spared from the line were engaged in moving the cycles back to the rear, and this saved the total loss of several; as it was some 90 cycles were so badly damaged as to be totally useless.

We had many casualties in this sector, as all the time the shelling and M.G. fire was intense.

Lieut. (A. Capt.) Dickeson, killed.

Lieuts. McLean and Branson, wounded.

Among the N.C.O.'s and men, Sergt. H. Gilchrist M.M., Privates R. H. Curtis, O. Fisher, A. Gold, D. Mulcahy, J. D. Welsh and H. R. Williams were killed or subsequently died of wounds.

The whole engagement cost the Unit 4 officers and 96 other ranks, besides 100 cycles.

On the 1st May the Battalion was relieved and moved out to Hillhoek (between Poperinghe and Abeele) where comfortable billets in huts were obtained. Here the Battalion remained till the 12th May, carrying on re-organisation and training, and enjoying a spell after the six weeks strenuous operations.

Decorations for gallantry were awarded the following N.C.O.'s and men —

M.M.	Sergt.	F. G. Matthews
	Sergt.	H. M. Carr
	Corpl.	F. C. Forrester
	Private	C. Brown
	Private	C. McLean
	Private	T. Nimmo
	Private	I. G. West
	Private	A. A. Close

Reinforcements to the number of 93 arrived on the 8th inst., also three officers from Infantry Units for attachment, viz., 2nd Lieuts. D. C. Griffiths, R. G. R. Sinclair, and E. Malcolm. The two latter did not remain long, rejoining their units a few days later.

On the 12th May the Battalion moved to Polinchove Area under orders received from Corps and went into billets at a village called RUMINGHEM, near Watten. The inhabitants were very kind to all ranks, who enjoyed their stay in this place.

2nd Lieut. Bloomfield (O.I.R.) joined the Battalion as an attached officer, and 2nd Lieut. A. H. Coe, M.M., left for England to embark for New Zealand on a tour of duty.

On the 17th May, Major Evans, D.S.O., returned from hospital and resumed command, and the same day the Battalion were attached to 2nd Army for cable burying with the French.

Major H. D. McHugh, M.C.
2nd. I/C N.Z. Cyclist Battalion.

CHAPTER XV.

WITH THE FRENCH AT MONT DES CATS.

On the 17th May Captain McHugh, M.C. (who was placed in charge of the cable laying) accompanied by Captains Richards and Comer, proceeded by motor to EECKE *via* Winnizeele to survey the routes and points which were to be connected by cable. Next day, the 18th, Nos. 1 and 2 Companies left Ruminghem for Winnizeele where they went into camp. The weather was perfect, and it was decided to start in the early morning, 4 a.m., allot each man a task 7 ft. x 7 ft. x 1½ft. and when that job was completed the rest of the day was given up to recreational training. Work was started next morning, 19th, and the going was good. The men proceeded to work on their cycles some six miles from the camp. The party told off for laying the cable preceded them by lorry. The work was generally completed by 9 a.m. and the men returned to camp by 10 a.m. Under these conditions, which the men thoroughly enjoyed, the work progressed rapidly on a daily average of 400 yards completed cable line. The companies were changed every six days, having two companies on work at cable and one at Battalion Headquarters, Ruminghem, for training purposes. The training consisted of the usual Company training and musketry practices on rifle ranges at MOULE.

Our work on cable was in the area taken over by the French, and our men received a great ovation from them, besides learning the ways and methods of our staunch allies. This work was continued until the 4th June, when our Corps was ordered to proceed south to near Amiens and to be there in reserve should the enemy attempt to continue his advance on the coast. On the morning of the 5th June Battalion Headquarters and No. 2 Company moved out and made a small forest near WIZERNES that night, where bivouacs were prepared. Nos. 1 and 3 Companies left Winnizeele the same morning and joined the Battalion there that evening. A move on was made next morning with destination Caupelle-Vielle near Fruges, a distance of roughly 25 miles being covered, and good time was made despite heat and dust. Billets awaited us, arranged by our advance party, and we soon settled down. Next morning we moved on again *via* FRUGES, ROUSSEAU-VILLE, AUCHY LE HESDIN, HESDIN, and over some steep hills to Wavans, our halting place. It was a long day—33 miles being covered.

Continuing next day we travelled over more hills to BOURDON through Flexicourt (4th Army Headquarters) and made our camp on the low-lying fields adjoining the SOMME River. Next day we moved on to Oissy, our final destination.

This treck from RUMINGHEM had taken us three full days and two half days, and the distance covered was about 90 miles.

This is not quick travelling for cyclists, who could do 40 miles a day easily, but we were hampered then by having slow horse transport, and the length of our day's journey had to be paced accordingly.

Visit to the Front by the Prime Minister, Hon. W. F. Massey and Sir Joseph Ward.

The Inspection.

The March Past.

The Prime Minister Addressing the Battalion.

Chapter XVI.

OISSY.

On arrlval at Oissy we were allotted the chateau grounds for our billetting area, and as tents were available made a camp in the wood adjoining the chateau. The weather was good and the men were comfortable, though several wet nights were encountered during our stay. On arrival we were joined by 2nd Lieuts. Greville, Rowland, Wylie, Randall, D.C.M., and Yorke, new officers for attachment. This brought our complement of officers to full strength.

Our stay at Oissy was for five weeks, during which the Battalion was trained in its job for open warfare. Several practice "stunts" were carried out in conjunction with the Mounted Regiment and an Armoured Car Battalion. The latter was entirely a new organisation, having eight armoured cars to the Battalion. The cars were armed with two Hotchkiss guns, one in each turret, going into action at 60 miles per hour and coming out at 25 miles per hour without turning the car, having a driver both front and rear. This unit was very mobile and where decent roads existed proved most valuable in the offensive and defensive. They were included in Corps Mounted Troops and our practice "stunts" with them were valuable and instructive.

In the chateau grounds there was a fine ornamental lake, and this was much used by all ranks for bathing and aquatic sports. The recreational portion of the training was not forgotten, and sports in conjunction with the Mounted Regiment were held on three occasions, together with a race meeting organised by Corps Headquarters.

A ten mile cycle race (on service machines) was held one evening and great interest was manifested by all ranks. The winner was Sergt. Sutherland, M.M., out of eighteen starters.

On the 14th June the Corps Commander, Lieut.-Gen. A. J. Godley, K.C.B., K.C.M.G., inspected the Corps and expressed himself very well pleased with the turnout. On the 3rd July we were visited by the Hon. W. J. Massey, Prime Minister, and the Hon. Sir J. G. Ward, Finance Minister, of New Zealand, who, after inspection of the Battalion and the Otago Mounted Rifles, briefly addressed the assembled troops. The party afterwards inspected the camp and then proceeded by cars to Paris.

On the 13th July, after spending some five weeks in the woods of Oissy, a rumour went around of a move, as it was said that the Corps was under orders to move. Preparations in anticipation of orders were made, and next morning (Sunday, 14th July) orders to entrain the Unit arrived at an early hour. The transport and two Companies were to entrain at Pont Remy at noon, and Battalion Headquarters and one Company at HANGEST at 3 p.m. for a destination then unknown.

Nos. 2 and 3 Companies under Capt. A. H. Richards left for Pont Remy and arrived in ample time to entrain. The transport, although a long march (10 miles) on heavy roads, was also on time. Battalion Headquarters and No. 1 Company arrived at Hangest at 1 p.m., and entrainment proceeded.

The Mounted Regiment were also entraining two squadrons at Pont Remy,, and one squadron (O.M.R).

The trains moved out at 7 p.m.; our destination was then given as somewhere east of PARIS. We travelled all night, the route being *via* EU-BEAUVAIS. The shorter route through AMIENS was not used owing to the enemy shelling the line. In the morning we stopped at CHARS for breakfast and on again to Paris, passing west of that city *via* VERSAILLES. At 5 p.m. we arrived at PONT SUR SEINE and detrained, billeting in that village for the night.

Next day orders arrived to move on to Vertus about 70 kilometers away in an easterly direction. The day was very hot, and many hills had to be climbed, consequently the going was slow and hard work. We stopped at VILLENEUX for lunch and made SEZANNE at 4 p.m., where billets were found for the night.

Next morning the Battalion moved forward early and arrived at VERTUS before lunch, and found our billets were at a small village named CHEVIGNY, three kilometers further on, where we were very comfortable.

The next morning we were ordered to move into Vertus, as French troops were allotted this village. On arrival we had great difficulty about accommodation, and on learning that Chevigny was not occupied (the French troops not having arrived) we returned and re-occupied our old billets.

CHAPTER XVII.

ON THE MARNE—MARFAUX.

On Friday, the 19th, while the Battalion rested, Major Evans was away all day in the direction of Reims on a reconnaissance of the forward positions, and returned with the information that the French troops and our Corps were attacking next morning, and that we were to move up to support the attackers if required. So on Saturday morning we moved out at 4 a.m. to AY, near Epernay, on the Marne River, arriving at our destination at 6 a.m. We stacked cycles on the roadside and waited there all day, ready to move forward if required. In Epernay, about two miles away, a large fire was burning, started by a bombardment from enemy long range guns. At 6 p.m. orders were received to bivouac for the night, so we moved to the canal bank at AY and settled down, all ranks enjoying a swim in the canal after a hot and dusty day.

On Sunday we stood to all day expecting orders, and at 6 p.m. they arrived with instructions for the Battalion to report to the 62nd Division at St. Imoges, on the top of the MONTAGNE de REIMS. At 9 p.m. we moved out, the C.O. going ahead to Divisional Headquarters, where he received orders to report to G.O.C. 186th Infantry Brigade at FME de ECUEIL. The Unit was met on the road and directed to its altered location. The destination was reached by midnight after a difficult ride along miles of indifferent roads through dense forests where the roads were full of troops, transport, motor lorries, etc. One of the boys had his leg broken through being run over.

Arriving at our destination we bivouacked in a small wood close to an Italian Heavy Battery and some Devon troops. Next morning we could see in the distance that once beautiful city of Reims, now utterly

AREO PHOTO OF MARFAUX.   MARNE, 23/7/18.

On the Marne—Marfaux

destroyed by the enemy's bombardment, and a mile or so to the east of us the battle was raging in earnest.

During the forenoon Major Evans and the Senior Officers went out with the G.O.C. of the 186th Brigade (Brig. Gen. Burnett) to look over some ground where the Battalion was to operate next day, and returned later with the news that the Battalion would move up to the assembly trenches that night and attack and capture the village of Marfaux at 6 a.m. next morning During the interval preparations were made. Cycles could not be used so were parked under cover from view, and at 11 p.m. that night the Battalion (less transport) moved off, arriving at and occupying the assembly trenches at 2 a.m.

Battalion Headquarters were established at a village named Pourcy, some 600 yards in rear, where Major Evans directed operations.

Marfaux, the Battalion's objective, is a small village on the right bank of the River ARDRE, and marks the limit of the enemy's advance on the 3rd of June, 1918. The capture of this village was attempted on the previous Saturday, but the troops on reaching the village had to retire under heavy fire, as it was untenable. A distance of 800 to 1,000 yards separated the assembly trenches from the village. Our force for the attack consisted of the Battalion and a small company of the 24th Hampshires, making a total of 340 all ranks.

During the remainder of the morning until zero hour there was intermittent shelling by the enemy and gas towards daybreak.

At 6 a.m. a creeping barrage was put down by the British, French and Italian Batteries, and the advance started in two waves. Our boys advanced under cover of the barrage and the first objective was reached on time but not before several casualties had occurred. The ground 300 yards in front of the objective sloped down from a crest which afforded no cover whatever. Enemy machine gunners took advantage of this and swept the ground with bullets until they were finally overtaken by the barrage and either dislodged or killed.

The village was "mopped up" and a number of prisoners, including a German doctor and Captain, were found in dugouts, who surrendered freely. In the dressing station were found two wounded British, who had been there since Saturday, and several wounded Germans.

In the meanwhile the second wave of the advance passed through the first and arrived at their objective line 300 yards in front of the village and consolidated in record time. A visual signal station was established at a point from which "all objectives taken" was sent back to Battalion Headquarters. The first wave, after mopping up the village, "dug in" 100 yards in rear of the first line in support.

So ended the battle of Marfaux. Our boys had done their job well, showing that dash and determination so well known of Colonial troops.

During the operation we captured 9 enemy Machine Guns and re-captured several French and our own Lewis Guns, a battery of 75's, and numerous souvenirs.

Our casualties were high. Among the officers were :

KILLED :

2nd Lieut. Griffith, D.C.
2nd Lieut. Rowland, A.E.M.

WOUNDED :

Captain Richards, A.H.
2nd Lieut. Greville, R.H.
2nd Lieut. Wylie, L.T.

Among the other ranks, the following were killed, or subsequently died of wounds received :—

Sergeant   Matthews, F.C., M.M.
Lance Sergeant Foulds, C.R.
Lance Corporals Foote, P.A. and Grindrod, C.

Privates Baker, F.   Chatwin, R. A.
          Hannan, F.   Johnson, H. J.
          Kloth, A. R.   Lindsay, H. J.
          McLaughlin, A. J.   McLeod, A. R.
          Mills, H.   Newman, L. A.
          Perry, A. J.   Sunmiss, F. A. H.
          Smith, A. E.   Smith, F. W. T.
          Turner, R. H.

and about 70 men wounded.

The stretcher bearers and medical orderlies deserve the greatest praise for the way they carried out their job. They worked unceasingly, though the day was exceptionally hot, and the carry back a long distance.

The officers who went forward with the advance and arrived at their objectives, Lieuts. Knubley, Blomfield and Yorke (the latter wounded but carried on) worked very hard, and were most energetic in caring for the wants of the men, caring little for themselves in their desire to see the job through.

C.S.M. Baker, M.M., was also conspicuous in his fine leadership after all his company officers became casualties.

For the next three days we held our line. The enemy did not "counter attack," though he sent over some strong patrols who met with a very warm reception.

On Friday night we came out into the Reserve line, the old assembly trenches. Captain McHugh, M.C., who returned from leave that day, taking over command of the line.

Next day a general advance was commenced towards BLINGY, by the Scottish and Yorkshire troops. We were withdrawn and sent back to our cycles to operate with the Corps Mounted Regiment in the advance.

Having obtained our cycles we returned to PRESLE FARM where we camped for the night, moving forward to to MARFAUX at daylight on Sunday morning. It had rained heavily during the night and the roads, with the traffic of guns, transport, etc., forward, were in an awful mess, making our progress very difficult.

We remained at MARFAUX all day, the Cavalry being out in front on patrols and reconnaissances.

On Monday night what was left of the Battalion was sent out under Captain McHugh, M.C., on a reconnaissance in force to the slopes of MONTAGNE de BLINGY. This patrol advanced 1,000 yards to a wood in front of our forward positions, captured a prisoner and gained a lot of valuable information.

On Wednesday the British troops in the sector were relieved by the French and we moved out, bivouacking in Bois de Talina for the night. Next morning we moved on to DIZY-MAGENTA, where we marched past Gen. A. Berthelot, Commander of the Fifth French Army, under whose command our Corps had been during the operation on the Marne. He issued a special army order of the day in reference to our work and gave all ranks in the Corps great praise.

The review over, we moved to the canal at AY, and in record time the canal was full of soldiers minus khaki, enjoying the first wash that many had had for ten days or so. We rested there for two hours and then on to MOUSSY, near EPERNEY, where billets were secured. We spent Friday and Saturday, the 2nd and 3rd August, at Moussy, resting and reorganising, for the Unit was reduced to small numbers.

On Sunday, 4th August, we received orders to return with the Corps to the north again and to entrain that night, men and cycles at OIRY and the transport at VERTUS. The transport left at 2 p.m. under Lieut. W. E. Randall, D.C.M., and the Battalion at 6 p.m.

Trains were late, and it was nearly morning before we left Oiry. We arrived at MARLES, E. of PARIS at 10 a.m., where a halt was made for breakfast; then on to PANTIN, N.E. of Paris, passing that city on the

THE ROAD TO MARFAUX.

THE BRITISH CEMETERY AT MARFAUX

Contains 800 graves, British, Australian and New Zealand soldiers, killed in the Valley of the Arde.

On the Marne—Marfaux

eastern side. Whilst at PANTIN we could hear the big shells from the German "Big Bertha" bursting near St. DENIS.

We continued our journey to the north and at 6 a.m. next morning arrived just N. of ABBEVILLE, near the mouth of the SOMME River. Our final destination by train was BRYAS, near ST. POL, where we detrained, and marched to billets at CONTEVILLE.

So ended our visit to CHAMPAGNE. The whole trip was an experience of value to us all, and if not for the fact of leaving so many of our dear comrades behind us, it would remain as a pleasant memory.

As a result of the good work done by officers and men, the following decorations were earned and awarded:

MILITARY CROSS :

Lieut.	H. C. J. Knubley
2nd Lieut.	E. H. Blomfield
2nd Lieut.	H. M. Yorke

D.C.M.

C.S.M.	W. H. Thomas

MILITARY MEDAL :

Sergeant	W. H. Thomas
Sergeant	H. E. Coates
Sergeant	F. A. Sutherland
Private	J. E. Shewry
Private	A. J. Byron
Private	A. McCulloch

The following French decorations were awarded :—

LEGION DE HONNEUR (CHEVALIER).

Major	C. H. Evans, D.S.O.

MEDAILLE MILITAIRE :

R.S.M.	A. Turner
Private	A. McIntosh

CROIX DE GUERRE :

Sergeant	W. Jamieson
Private	·C. D. McLaren

WIRE].

O.C. 22. CORPS CYCLISTS BTN/.

c/o 62nd Division.

Following from 22nd Corps begins aaa. The Corps Commander wishes to express his appreciation of the good work done by the N.Z. Cyclists Btn. during the present operations, and desires you to convey his congratulations to Major Evans and all ranks of his command on their gallantry and success in the attack aaa ends aaa For necessary action.
Recd. 26/7/18.,

6 p.m. C.D.E.

22nd Corps Mounted Troops.

SPECIAL ORDER

BY

LIEUTENANT-GENERAL SIR A. J. GODLEY, K.C.B., K.C.M.G.
Commanding XXII. Corps.

The following order of the day by General Bertholot commanding Fifth (French) Army, together with the Corps Commanders' reply to it, are published for the information of all ranks.

The Corps Commander wishes this Order to be distributed as widely as possible, and to be read out on parade, and takes this opportunity of expressing to the Commanders, Staffs and All Ranks of the 51st (Highland) and the 62nd (West Riding) Divisions, and all the Corps Troops, his thanks for the loyal assistance and support that he has had from them during the recent arduous operations.

He takes this opportunity of again expressing his admiration of the conspicuous valour and endurance of the troops, and trusts that it may be his good fortune to have them again under his command in any future operations.

      (Sgd.) A. M. de la VOYE,
            D.A. and Q.M.G.

Headquarters,
  31/7/1918.

TRANSLATION.

Vme Armée

        Q.G., July 30th, 1918.

Etat Major
3me Bureau ORDER OF THE DAY No. 63.
No. 1863/3.

Now that the XXII. British Corps has received orders to leave the Fifth (French) Army, the Army Commander expresses to all the thanks and admiration which the great deeds, that it has just accomplished, deserve.

The very day of its arrival, feeling in honour bound to take part in the victorious counter-attack which had just stopped the enemy's furious onslaught on the Marne, and had begun to hurl him back in disorder to the North, the XXII. Corps, by forced marches and with minimum opportunity for reconnaissance, threw itself with ardour into the battle.

By constant efforts, by harrying and by driving back the enemy for ten successive days, it has made itself master of the Valley of the ARDRE, which it has so freely watered with its blood.

Thanks to the heroic courage and proverbial tenacity of the British, the continued efforts of this brave Army Corps have not been in vain.

21 officers and 1,300 other ranks taken prisoner, 140 Machine Guns, and 40 Guns captured from an enemy, four of whose Divisions have been successively

broken and repulsed; the Upper Valley of the ARDRE, with its surrounding heights to the north and south, reconquered; such is the record of the British share in the operations of the Fifth Army.

Highlanders under the orders of General Carter-Campbell, commanding the 55th Division; Yorkshire lads under the orders of General Braithwaite, commanding the 62nd Division; Australian and New Zealand Mounted Troops; all officers and men of the XXII. Army Corps, so ably commanded by General Sir A. Godley, you have added a glorious page to your history.

MARFAUX, CHAUMUZY, MONTAGNE de BLIGNY—all these famous names will be written in letters of gold in the annals of your regiments.

Your French comrades will always remember with emotion your splendid gallantry and your perfect fellowship in the fight.

"BERTHELOT,"
le General Commandant,
la Vme Armée.

SPECIAL ORDER
BY
Lieutenant General Sir A. J. Godley, k.c.b., k.c.m.g.
Commanding XXII. Corps.

The Corps Commander has been desired by the General-Officer-Commanding Fifth (French) Army to express his great satisafction at the appearance and bearing of the troops which he reviewed this morning. The Corps Commander wishes to add his appreciation of the excellent turn-out, good march discipline and smartness of the representative detachments of the Corps Mounted Troops, 51st (Highland) Division and 62nd (West Riding) Division, and to thank them for the evid-

THE CORPS GUIDES, SUPPLIED BY THE BATTALION.

REVIEW OF 51ST. DIVISION XXII. CORPS
By General Berthelot, 5th Armie Francaise, 1/8/18.
Dizy, Maggenta, Marne.

ent pains which they they had taken, though only just out of the battle, to so worthily uphold the credit of the British Army before the French Generals and Staffs.

(sd.) A.M. de la VOYE,
D.A. and Q.M.G.,
XXII. Corps.

Headquarters
1/8/18.

62nd (W.R.) Divn.
31st July, 1918.

XXII. Corps "G."

I have the honour to bring to the notice of the Corps Commander the services of the Cyclist Battalion, Corps Troops XXII. Army Corps, under the command of Major C. H. Evans, D.S.O., which have been attached to the Division under my command during the recent operations. Nothing could have been better than the fighting qualities displayed by, or the valour and endurance of, all ranks not only during the action of 23rd July, but throughout the subsequent fighting.

I desire also to bring to the notice of the Corps Commander, the services of the Corps Mounted Troops, under Lieut.-Colonel Hindhaugh, who did valuable service throughout the time they were attached to the Division under my command. The men shewed enterprise and bravery while working in a country difficult for Cavalry. The patrols were boldly handled and sent back useful and accurate information.

(sgd.) W. P. BRAITHWAITE,
Major-General
Commanding 62nd (West Riding) Division.

Headquarters,
31/7/18.

G.O.C. 62nd. (W.R.)

Dear Evans,—Now that you have left my Brigade I should like to thank both you and your men for the splendid work you did at MARFAUX. You had a nasty job to do and could not have done it better. Would you please let your officers and men know how much we appreciated all the help you gave us at a very trying time.

Yours sincerely,

(sgd.)   J. S. BENNETT,
Brig.-General.

(For orders).

185th Brigade.

CHAPTER XVIII.

THE SECOND BATTLE OF THE SOMME.

Reinforcements arrived for us at Conteville to the number of 60 ; also 2nd Lieuts. Bowron and Evans. We were also favoured by the attachment of a Padre, Captain Rev. L. A. Knight. Up to the present time our spiritual welfare had not been attended to except occasionally by Padres belonging to other Units, so we welcomed his arrival with pleasure.

2nd Lieut. T H. Dickinson, who had been acting Adjutant in the absence of A. Capt. G. Clark Walker, to Hospital, sick, went for a six weeks' course of instruction to 1st Army Infantry School, Hardelot, and Lieut.-Quartermaster C. G. G. Johnson, was appointed to carry on his duties in his absence.

Lieut.-Gen. Sir A. J. Godley, who had taken over the duties of the G.O.C. III. Corps (on sick leave) sent for his Corps Mounted Troops on the 20th August, and we accordingly packed up and moved south at 8 p.m., arriving at REOMAISNIL, our halting place, at midnight, the transport arriving three hours later

We continued our march next evening, starting at 6 p.m., arriving at Villers-Bocage (where 3rd Corps Headquarters were situated) at 9 p.m. and bivouacked in an orchard.

Our retaliatory push had commenced to regain the ground lost in March and April, and up to the present good reports were received, and the arrival of bands of German prisoners, told us that the first phase of the advance was successful.

During the forenoon of next day we received orders to move forward in the direction of ALBERT. No. 1 Coy., under Captain McHugh, M.C., was detailed to report to a work under orders of 18th Division, the rest of the Battalion to go into bivouac at BOIS de ESCARDONNEUSE and await orders.

No. 1 Company left at 1 p.m. to report to 54th Infantry Brigade (18th Division) near Albert, the rest of the Battalion proceeding *via* QUERRIEU to LA HOUSSOYE, where it obtained billets in abandoned and ruined houses.

Next day, the 24th August, 1918, No. 2 Company, under Temp. Capt. Blomfield, M.C., and No. 3 Company, under Temp. Capt. Knubley, M.C., were detached and sent to report to 58th Division at HEILLY and 12th Division at RIBEMONT respectively for employment in reconnaissance and patrol work.

The description and report on the Companies' work follows.

Captain H. D. McHugh, M.C., O.C., No. 1 Company, reports as under :—

On the 22nd August the Company left the Battalion at VILLERS BOCAGE, and proceeded to near Albert, where the Company occupied some trenches and dugouts by the road side, the O.C, reporting personally to the G O.C. Fifty-fourth Infantry Brigade. Captain McHugh was then given orders that the Company would be used for the purposes of reconnaissance and patrol work to supply a steady source of information to the G.O.C. Brigades attached to. On the 23rd, Sergeant H. M. Carr M.M., was despatched with a patrol to ascertain the enemy positions at La BOISSELLE, and successfully carried out his mission. The same evening Lieut. Randall, D.C.M., and a patrol proceeded to the left of the Divisional front on a similar mission, and obtained the necessary information. On the 25th the Company was ordered to follow up the retiring enemy and moved out as an advanced guard to Longueval. The enemy was met with in considerable force at MAMETZ Wood and the advance held up. Nevertheless valuable information was obtained for Brigade by flanking movements. The advance continued each day when our patrols were on the heels of the enemy. On the 29th, forward to Combles, under full view and heavy M.G. fire, a reconnaissance in force made a dash and succeeded in reaching COMBLES and obtained very reliable information. The following day patrols were sent forward in three directions towards SAILLY, SAILLISEL and RANCOURT, and good reports sent in. From 2nd to 5th September, operating in the direction of St. Pierre Vaast and Vaux Woods, where the enemy made a stand, our patrols gained very useful information, being at times 2,000 yards in advance of our attacking infantry. Reconnaissances were daily continued until the 12th September, where PEIZIERE had been reached by that time.

On the above date the Company was withdrawn to join the Battalion. For the last 22 days they had been employed continually on reconnaissance, and in every case the patrols succeeded in gaining their objectives and in securing the special information asked for.

Captain McHugh in his report to the C.O. states :—

"I cannot praise the Company enough for the loyal support they have given me. The latest joined men worked with the older hands and soon acquired the principles of patrol work. Splendid work was carried out by the N.C.O.'s, who were my chief support, with so many new men. My officers, Lieuts. Cody and Randall, D.C.M., have had the bulk of the work to do, and I cannot praise them too highly. They had some very tough corners to investigate, and did their job thoroughly.

"The valuable work done by Sergt. Carr, M.M., Midgley, Brown and Lance Sergt. Ryan, cannot be passed by in these lines ; their coolness in tight coners, and daring on patrol work earned for them the praise of officers on Divisional and Brigade Staffs we have been attached to."

The Corps Commander directed a letter of appreciation of the work done by the advance guard to Brig.-Gen. Wood, the A.G. Commander, and the Brigade Major of the 55th Infantry Brigade wrote to Captain McHugh as follows :—

> "General Wood has directed me to inform you how delighted he was with all the work done by your command during the period attached to him. Reconnaissances ordered were always carried out quickly, and absolutely valuable information obtained and good reports sent back. He hopes that you will be attached to his Brigade in any future operations he may be entrusted with."

T. Capt. E. H. Blomfield, M.C., O.C., No. 2 Company, reports as under :—

On the 24th August the Company was ordered to report to the 58th Division, when operating on the right of the Corps front, and the O.C. Company reported to Divisional Headquarters at the Heilly Chateau, and was ordered to take his Company in the vicinity of HAPPY VALLEY near BRAY SUR SOMME. The Company left the Battalion billets at 10 p.m., and travelling by moonlight arrived at 1.30 a.m. at its destination, where good quarters had been found in German dugouts by an advance party. The Company remained in this place all day, and next morning were ordered forward to the Citadel on FRICOURT-BRAY Road. It had rained during the night, and the roads were in a very bad mess, necessitating the cycles being carried for a considerable part of the way. Sergt. Hughes, in charge of a patrol, had been sent forward, and had been out and working with the Northumberland Hussars, and had done some good work and gained valuable information. At 10 p.m. that night, 26th August, we were engaged with D Squadron A.L.H. in holding the line with Lewis guns south and west of Maricourt. 2nd Lieut. Bowron was

The Second Battle of the Somme

in charge of the guns, and his teams went over the top with the 3rd London Infantry next morning at dawn. Sergt. Coats and three men were wounded in the advance A patrol under 2nd Lieut. Ewan was sent out N. and N.E. of MARICOURT and obtained useful information.

This work continued without cessation until the night of the 28th, when patrols were withdrawn to Company Headquarters, and remained until 2 p.m. on the 29th, when the Company was ordered to move forward and occupy positions in front line. This, however, was altered, and the Company remained in reserve at BATTERY COPSE.

Patrols were sent out and kept busy obtaining information for Brigades and Division. On the 31st patrols were out all day in the direction of MARRIERS Wood and operated in front of our Infantry. One patrol captured 11 prisoners.

On the 3rd September the Company was transferred to 74th Division and moved to dugouts in MARRIERS Wood. There was little doing until the 6th when the Company again moved to a new position south o BOUCHAVESNES ; remained in this Camp doing small patrol work till next day, when we moved again to near AZIECOURT. Nothing further eventuated on the front to require the Company's services, as the Infantry had been unable to get forward. On the 12th September orders were received to rejoin Battalion at COMBLES, so the Company moved out and arrived at the latter place at 3.30 p.m.

During the period the Company was on detachment its work was of high order and the difficulties of roads, long distance, wire and enemy fire of all sorts were overcome and the object of the stunt, whether it was reconnaissance, defence or advance, was, without exception, carried out to the letter.

The officers were all new in their positions. T. Captain E. H. Blomfield, M.C., had only had command a month, and the two subalterns, 2nd Lieuts. F. L.

Bowron and J. F. Ewan had only just joined the Battalion. Still they took to the work as in manner born and earned high praise from the Divisional and Brigade Commanders. The N.C.O.'s were mostly newly appointed—many of the men counted their service with the Battalion by days. Nevertheless the aim of all was to give good service and they amply succeeded in their desire, for nothing could be finer than the work done by the other ranks.

T. Capt. H. C. J. Knubley, M.C., O C., No. 3 Company, reports:—

The Company was attached for work under a Division—in this case the 12th—a Welsh Division, and on the evening of the 24th August the O.C. Company reported at RIBEMONT to Divisional Headquarters and the Company went into bivouac for the night, along with B Squadron 4th A.L.H., with whom the Company worked throughout the operations.

Next morning at 3 a.m. orders were received to follow up the enemy's retirement which had started during the night. Accordingly the Company moved off *via* MEAULTE to the high ground between MONTEBAN and CARNOY near MAMETZ. The enemy was met with and the Company and L.H. dismounted for action. A lively little fight ensued in which we came off best, killing several and taking prisoners. It was here that Private W. G Cavenett performed a very plucky action. An enemy machine gun in POMMIERS Redoubt was annoying us and he and others were told off to silence it. Cavenett alone worked round the rear and, ignoring the heavy machine gun fire, rushed the position single handed bayonetted three of the garrison and took one man prisoner, the remainder of the garrison escaping. It was a very plucky action and earned for this soldier the cheers of his comrades and the award of the D.C.M.

The Company held their position till 5.30 p.m. when the 35th Infantry Brigade went through and took the ridge (MONTEBAN). The Company then withdrew to VILLE sur ANCRE, where they bivouacked for the night.

Later orders were received transferring the Company from the 35th to the 37th Brigade and ordering a concentration at CARNOY at 6.0 a.m. the following morning. The Infantry were attacking MARICOURT and had a stiff fight. The Company, being reserve, were not used, but got a good gassing from the enemy before they withdrew to their bivouac.

On the 29th, a further change took place, the 47th Division taking over from the 12th Division, and the Company attached to 142nd Brigade. The Company was not used, as the enemy was putting up a stiff fight at PRIEZ Farm and Cavalry and Cyclists could not get out.

At 8.0 a.m., the 30th, the Company moved to LE FORET MAREPAS, and took position on high ground, over-looking where they held on till relieved by Infantry in the evening. The first and only casualty occurred in this sector, Private Thacker being so badly wounded by a shell that he subsequently died. Private Shand, the Battalion nightingale, was wounded at the same time.

On the 31st August the Company was moved forward to MARICOURT, and remained in reserve till next night when 2nd Lieut. Nicholson and 20 men were sent to the 24th Londons to act as flank guard, during their advance from PRIEZ Farm, which they had captured with 170 prisoners. The party moved out at 2.0 a.m., 4th September, and "hopped over" with the 24th Londons at 5.30 a.m., carrying out their job all day and remaining entrenched that night and all next day, being relieved at 5.0 p.m. The officer and his party received the thanks of the G.O.C. 142nd Brigade for their good work. It was here that we lost our only prisoner to the enemy, Private J. Fisher being captured whilst on patrol. (He was, however, released after the Armistice.)

On the 4th September an inter Division change took place, the 58th relieving the 47th, and the Company was transferred. No operations took place, but the Company bivouac was moved forward to BOIS de HEM, where very good quarters were secured.

Received orders to report at 5.30 a.m. next day, the 5th, to 141st Brigade at BOUCHAVESNES, and on doing this were ordered to send a patrol to BOIS de EPINETTE and AZIECOURT, to ascertain the position with regard to our troops and the enemy. This was successfully accomplished, the enemy having left. On this information the Infantry moved up and took possession of the village of LIERMONT. The patrol returned at 6.30 p.m.

On the 6th, no orders being received in regard to operations, the Company moved forward again to MOISLAINS, where quarters were obtained in what was a British C.C.S. prior to March, '18. The CANAL du NORD was close by and all ranks indulged in the luxury of a swim—the first for many days.

On the 7th there was nothing doing, except the supply of Cyclist runners between the Brigade and Battalions.

On the 8th, the Division the Company was working under was withdrawn from the line, and the Company was sent back to the Battalion near MAMETZ to be in Corps reserve.

In common with Nos. 1 and 2 Companies, this Company earned the highest praise for its faithful and complete work. Its officers, like No. 2, were new to their positions. T. Capt. Knubley, M.C., had only been Company Commander since the battle of MARFAUX, and 2nd Lieut. E.C.E. Nicholson only joined the day before going into action. Nevertheless, their work was of high order; and they were ably and faithfully assisted by the N.C.O.'s and men of the Company, who, to a man, worked hard amid trying and unpleasant conditions in a manner characteristic of THE NEW ZEALAND CYCLIST CORPS.

The Second Battle of the Somme

After the departure of Nos. 2 and 3 Companies on 24th August, Battalion Headquarters with Transport settled down. The Companies' packs were all stored away and the only personnel left were a few sick, besides the Headquarters Signallers and details. The C.O., Adjutant, and acting Q.M. (2nd Lieut. D. H. Evans) and the Padre were the only officers with Battalion Headquarters.

The C.O. visited one or more of the Companies daily, and as the line was advancing rapidly the distance of travel increased. On the 7th September, Battalion Headquarters moved forward and occupied some German dugouts near MAMETZ, and again on the 10th moved still further to BOIS DOUAGE near COMBLES, where German dugouts were again used.

Consequent on the Corps front being held by two Divisions, one Company (No. 3) was withdrawn from the front line on the 8th September, and joined the Battalion at MAMETZ and held in Corps reserve. A much appreciated consignment of gift parcels from the Lady Liverpool Fund arrived, and were very welcome to the boys in a part of France where such foods and comforts as were contained in these parcels were quite unobtainable. The receipt of these gifts from the women of New Zealand were always most acceptable and the thanks of the soldiers are heartily given to the donors.

Lieut.-Gen. Sir A. J. Godley, K.C.B., K.C.M.G., our Corps Commander, who had been commanding 3rd Corps during the absence of Lieut-Gen. Butler, on relinquishing command of the Corps sent a letter to all Units in the Corps, in which he expressed his appreciation of the work done during the advances E. of ALBERT from the 11th August till the 12th September, and thanked all troops for their support and assistance. *Inter alia* he says : "The Mounted Troops and Cyclists of the 3rd and 22nd Corps have rendered conspicuous service in patrolling, reconnaissance and liaison work."

The advance referred to covered 22 miles on a 4¼ mile front (Corps front) and recaptured 28 towns and villages, 7,300 prisoners, of whom 146 were officers, 43 guns and numerous M.G.'s, T.M.'s and stores.

On the 12th September our Corps Commander having returned to resume Command of our Corps (22nd) we received orders to return also, and having concentrated the detached Companies, packed up once more, and at 9.0 a.m. on the 13th September, left COMBLES on route march northwards, our first day's journey being to COUIN. As the roads in the old SOMME battlefield, POISIERES, etc., were in bad repair, we went the longer way round *via* ALBERT, BOUZINCOURT, BETRANCOURT, and made our destination in good time despite the heavy head wind.

Continuing next day we found our final destination in STEWART CAMP, about 1½ miles west of ARRAS, on the ST. POL Road. The Camp was composed of N.B. Huts, and there was splendid horse standings which were occupied by the Corps Mounted Regiment, who were also with us in the Camp.

The good work done by Officers, N.C.O.'s and men in the advance on the SOMME in August and September, were rewarded by the following decorations being awarded :—

M.C.	2nd Lieut.	F. L. Bowron
D.C.M.	Private	W. G. Cavenett
Bar to M.M.	Sergeant	H. M. Carr
M.M.	Corporal	I. W. Weston
M.M.	Sergeant	F. E. Brown
M.M.	Private	F. Barlow
M.M.	Lance.-Sergt.	R. Ryan
M.M.	Sergeant	H. L. Midgley

CHAPTER XIX.

ARRAS—MONS.

By 14th September, 1918, the Unit was comfortably settled down, the Camp being well suited for our requirements.

The Corps front extended from GAVRELLE, N.E. of ARRAS, to a point near L'ECLUSE on ARRAS-CAMBRAI Road, and the nature of our duties requiring a knowledge of the front, parties of officers and the N.C.O.'s were attached to Lovatt's Scouts (who man the Army O.P.'s) in order that they might become acquainted with the position of the roads, trenches, etc. A number of men under 2nd Lieut. Bowron were also sent to guard Railway tunnels and bridges on AUBIGNY ARRAS railway. Another detachment of Lieut. Highet and 27 men was sent to 11th Division for reconnaissance and liaison work.

On the 16th September Captain H. D. McHugh, who was commanding the Battalion in the absence of the C.O., Major Evans, D.S.O., in England on duty, was sent to hospital suffering from gas burns received on the Somme, Captain G. L. Comer taking over command of the Battalion.

It being found that the name this Unit was known by, viz., XXII. Corps Cyclist Battalion was confusing, it was decided by Headquarters that in future, the Battalion, being a purely N.Z. Unit, should be known as :—

"NEW ZEALAND CYCLIST BATTALION."

On the 6th October the Battalion was inspected by G.O.C. 22nd Corps (Lieut.-Gen. Sir A. J. Godley, K.C.B., K.C.M.G.) who expressed himself pleased with the turn-out and smartness displayed.

The victorious advances being made on our immediate front foretold a move forward, and on the 10th October a warning order came that the Battalion was to be ready to move on short notice. Next day at noon the order came, and at 1.0 p.m. the Battalion moved out with its destination BOURLON. This village was reached at 6.0 p.m. after a trying march, owing to the traffic on the roads and bad going, it being necessary to push the cycles the greater part of the way.

On arrival billets were found in this town, which was very much damaged by shell fire, and next morning two Platoons of No. 1 Company were sent out to Divisions in the line to act as Scouts, etc., Lieut. D. G. Cody going with his platoon to 49th Division and 2nd Lieut. W. E. Randall, D.C.M., to 51st (Highland) Division.

That afternoon the remainder of the Battalion was ordered forward to RAMILLIES, north of CAMBRAI, and after a particularly trying march, the cycles having to be pushed all the way, arrived at 9.15 p.m., and after some difficulty found billets ; this village, having been the scene of heavy fighting two days earlier, was in ruins.

Next morning at 10.0 a.m. orders were received to send out all available fighting men to increase platoons with 49th and 51st Divisions to Company strength. This was done and Battalion Headquarters and transport was left at RAMILLIES.

Major Evans returned from duty in United Kingdom on the 14th instant, resumed command of the Battalion.

On the 16th October all personnel of No. 1 Company were withdrawn from Divisions, leaving No. 2 Company (T. Capt. Blomfield, M.C.) with 49th Division and No. 3 Company (Capt. Comer) with 51st Division.

These Companies continued with above and other Divisions until the Armistice was signed on the 11th November, 1918, and their doings are recorded separately.

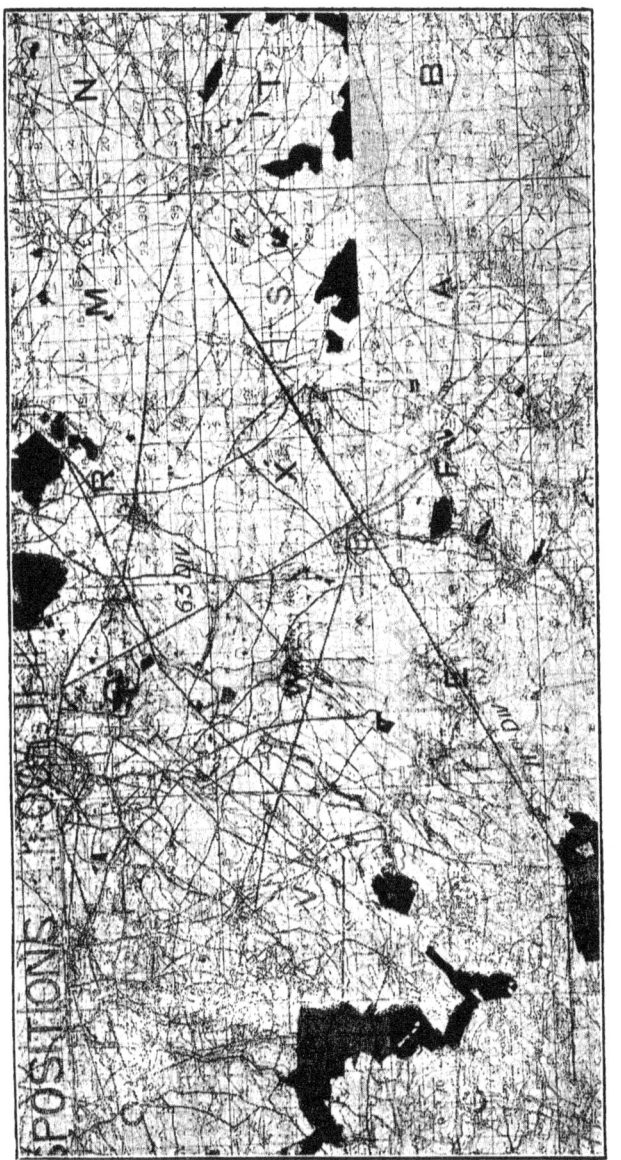

DISPOSITIONS OF THE XXII. CORPS, 11/11/18.

NARRATIVE OF No. 1 COMPANY, 12/10/18.-11/11/18.

At BOURLON on 12/10/'18, at 6 a.m., orders were received for two platoons to move out for attachment to Divisions operating in advance on the Corps fronts. Accordingly Lieut. D. G. Cody, with his platoon, went to 49th Division, and 2nd Lieut. W. E. Randall, with his platoon, to 51st Division. Both Divisions were at ESCAUDOEVRES near CAMBRAI. The roads were particularly bad, and very congested with the traffic necessary to an advancing army, and riding was impossible, the cycles having to be pushed all the way—a heavy task with a full pack up.

On arrival at Divisional Headquarters it was found that Divisions were moving to NAVES, and the two platoons moved to that village and billetted.

Next day Lieut. Cody's platoon was engaged as runners between Division (51st) Headquarters and the forward Brigades.

Lieut. Randall's platoon (with 49th Division) was similarly engaged, also finding patrols along NAVES-VILLERS Road. Whilst so engaged Lieut. Randall was slightly wounded and returned to Battalion Headquarters at RAMILLIES, Sergt. F. E. Brown, M.M., taking charge of the platoon.

This platoon received "special mention" from the Brigadier 147th Infantry Brigade for its excellent work. This sort of work went on until the 17th October, when the two platoons were ordered back to rejoin their Company at Battalion Headquarters, where the Company remained in reserve until the 28th October, when it was sent to THIANT to relieve No. 3 Company, then attached to 51st Division (152nd Infantry Brigade).

On the 29th, the 49th Division took over the 51st Division front and the Company was transferred to former Division.

On the 30th and 31st the Company supplied runners for Brigades, and the Officers and N.C.O.'s made reconnaissances of the country forward in view of the continuation of the advance on the 1st November. The village of THIANT was well shelled by the enemy, but no casualties to our men resulted.

Early on the morning of the 1st November the attack commenced with certain objectives, and our orders were that on those objectives being gained we were to push out strong patrols (in conjunction with the Corps Cavalry) and exploit the successes gained.

2nd Lieut. Greville with No. 1 Platoon was attached to the 146th Infantry Brigade and moved forward at 5.45 a.m. from THIANT to FAMARS, where cycles were left, as roads were bad and shelling was heavy. This platoon was heavily engaged by Machine Gun fire near AULNOY, but did good work in obtaining information, finally returning to Company Headquarters at 9.30 p.m.

No. 2 Platoon, under 2nd Lieut. C. C. Southey, M.M., worked forward on the left of 147th Brigade and near SAULTAIN, engaged three enemy field gun teams engaged in removing some light guns. The Lewis gun, worked by Lance Corporal Wharton and Private M McMeeking, shot the teams and forced the gunners to take shelter and kept them there until the platoon had to withdraw, owing to our Infantry having withdrawn. When withdrawing Lieut. Southey saw an enemy counter attack coming, so he again got his gun into action, the N.C.O. and man (Wharton and McMeeking) working the gun to such effect that the counter attack was stopped ; the party maintained their positions until dark and then withdrew to Brigade Headquarters, where the Brigadier met them and made very complimentary reference to the excellent work done by them.

2nd Lieut. Southey was afterwards awarded the M.C., and the two gunners (Lance Corporal Wharton and Private D. McMeeking) the M.M., for their gallantry and devotion to duty, on the Brigadier's recommendation.

On the 2nd November the Company was attached to 148th Infantry Brigade, but was not used.

NARRATIVE OF No. 2 COMPANY

On the 3rd the Company was ordered to report to MONCHAUX to XXII. Corps Mounted Troops, and finally, after much difficulty, owing to bad roads, made FAMARS. Next morning moved on to SAULTAIN and billetted there, and beyond finding a few runners was not used.

On the 6th moved to SEBOURQUIAUX and billetted. On the 8th moved out in direction of AUTREPPE on reconnaissance and patrol work, and the men had a very difficult and unpleasant time owing to heavy rain and bad roads. However their work was most successful, and all patrols accomplished their missions. When preparing to move from SEBOURQUIAUX, the enemy shelled the village, and a shell bursting near by wounded Sergt. Midgley so badly that he subsequently died.

On the 10th instant Captain H. D. McHugh, M.C., rejoined the Company, having been away in hospital for a brief period suffering from gas burns.

The Company was on that day ordered to FAYT le FRANC to report to 56th Division, by whom it was employed in controlling and directing traffic, and on various duties. Subsequently it was moved on to ATHIS where it remained until hostilities ceased.

On the 12th instant orders were received by the Company to rejoin the Battalion, but owing to location being incorrectly given, it marched to HARVENGT, where the Corps Mounted Troops had their Headquarters, and from there was directed to AULNOIS, the location of the Battalion.

NARRATIVE OF No. 2 COMPANY, 12/10/18-11/11/18

On the 12th October, the Company, with the rest of the Battalion, arrived at RAMILLIES late at night from BOURLON. On the morning of the 13th, under command of T. Capt. E. H. Blomfield (who had with him Lieuts. Highet and Knubley, M.C.) the Company marched out to IWUY and reported to 51st Division. Billets were found, and next morning the Officer Commanding was instructed to report to 152nd Infantry Brigade, who ordered a change of location to NAVES.

On the 16th Captain A. H. Richards, who was wounded at MARFAUX in July, rejoined, and took over command of the Company. There being no offensive operations, the Company was employed with the D.A.C., 51st Division, loading ammunition, and between whiles indulged in football, though the village was under shellfire.

Meantime the 49th Division had taken over the 51st Division and the Company was transferred. On the 19th, the 4th Division relieved the 49th and again the Company transferred, and it was under orders of the 4th Division that 2nd Lieut. Bowron's Platoon went to the 10th Brigade, and 2nd Lieut. J. F. Ewen's platoon to 11th Brigade, who were at VILLERS EN CAUCHIES on the 19th instant.

These two platoons were employed by the respective Brigades on patrol and reconnaissance duties in front of the advancing infantry, and were constantly on the move forward.

On the 21st 2nd Lieut. Ewen's platoon moved to HASPRES, and from there made a reconnaissance of MONCHAUX village. In carrying out their mission 2nd Lieut. Ewen was wounded. Nevertheless the party carried on and obtained the required information, Lance Corporal Hasting and Private Prenderville giving very good service in bringing their wounded officer back over difficult ground.

On the 22nd 2nd Lieut. L. H. Browne and his platoon relieved 2nd Lieut. Ewen's men, who had had a very strenuous time. 2nd Lieut. Bowron's men had meantime been operating forward on SAULZOIR with success.

On the 23rd the Company moved its Headquarters (with the Division) to ASVENES-LE-SEC. Captain

NARRATIVE OF NO. 2 COMPANY

Richards left the Company at this place, he having been granted a "course" in England in Staff duties, and Lieut. E. H. Blomfield again took over the Company.

On the 25th, 2nd Lieut. Browne moved up to SAULZOIR and from there made a very successful reconnaissance of the village of ARTRES and the surrounding country, ascertaining enemy dispositions and enabling our artillery to deal effectively with them. Nos. 5 and 6 Platoons (2nd Lieuts. Bowron and Ewen) moved to LA TRAVISE, and the Company Headquarters remained at ASVENES-LE-SEC.

No further operations were undertaken until the 1st November, when the Company moved to HASPRES, Nos. 4 and 5 Platoons being sent on ahead to reconnoitre ground near PREASEAU and towards CURGIES, but owing to strong enemy opposition this patrol did not accomplish its mission. Next day the advance continued, and the Company Headquarters moved forward, the Platoons with Brigade continuing their work and in succession reconnoitring and occupying ARTRES and CURGIES with the Infantry. The going for cyclists over all this country proved very difficult owing to bad roads and the frequently met mine craters at road junctions.

On the 7th the Company moved to ROISIN and was engaged in operations with a Lincoln Regiment towards AUTREPPE which were quite successful. Lieut. Bowron was wounded in this advance.

The Company, its mission finished, withdrew to ROISIN, and next day moved again to AUTREPPE, and on the 9th to AULNOIS. Patrols were sent on ahead to ascertain the position, and this village was found unoccupied. The patrols received a great reception from civilians as each village was reached, particularly at BLAREGNIES.

On the 10th the Company moved on to QUEVY LE GRAND, at which village the 33rd Infantry Brigade (Brig.-Gen. Spring) had its Headquarters.

On the 11th November instructions were received from G.O.C. 189th Brigade that Armistice would start at 11.0 a.m., and that the Company was to proceed to GIVRY and form a right flank for 189th Brigade. This was done, and at 11.0 a.m., when the Great War finished, this Company was in battle position in the front line. Outposts were established and maintained on the night of 11th-12th November. On the morning of the 12th, orders were received to rejoin Battalion at AULNOIS.

NARRATIVE OF No. 3 COMPANY, 13/10/18-11/11/18

On the 13th October the Company under command of Captain G. L. Comer, moved from RAMILLIES to IWUY, and reported to G.O.C. 51st Division. Not being required, billets were secured for the night. Next day moved to NAVES. Lieut. Knubley, M.C., took over command from Captain Comer, who returned to Battalion Headquarters sick.

The Company was not used except as working parties until the 18th, when patrols were sent forward to ASVENES LE SAC.

On the 19th moved to IWUY again, and at 5.0 p.m. a platoon was sent forward along the Valenciennes Road as scouts for the Brigade (153rd) which was advancing.

On the 20th moved to PAVE de VALENCIENNES, one platoon being sent to each of Infantry Battalions in the line as Scouts. Their work merited a message of appreciation from the Brigadier, who was very pleased with the resource and dash displayed by the Scouts.

On the 21st the Company moved to DOUCHY, and at 8.30 a.m. three patrols were sent out in the direction of VALENCIENNES to locate enemy. The patrols were respectively under Lieut. Highet and Corporals I. W. Weston, M.M., and C. Gerrard, and all did good work, resulting in the Brigadier expressing himself very pleased with the reports.

The Battalion Flag.

Official Entry into Mons, 15/11/18.
N.Z. Cyclists in the van.

O.M.R. AND CYCLISTS' COMBINED FOOTBALL TEAM.

CYCLIST BATTALION FOOTBALL TEAM.

NARRATIVE OF No. 3 COMPANY

On the 22nd one platoon (Lieut. H. A. Highet) was sent to NOVELLES and the remainder of the Company moved to ASVENES LE SEC where a brief rest was obtained.

On the 24th the Company moved to NOVELLES (to 153rd Infantry Brigade) and afterwards to DOUCHY again. 2nd Lieut. C. C. Southey, M.M., reported with a platoon to 6th Argyle and Sutherland Highlanders at THIANT for patrol duty but not being required returned to the Company.

On the 28th No. 1 Company, which was in reserve at RAMILLIES, moved in relief of No. 3 Company, which returned to RAMILLIES for a rest.

The Company remained with Battalion Headquarters, moving on the 3rd November to HASPRES and from there on to ARTRES for attachment to 33rd Infantry Brigade. On the 4th November, moved on again to CURGIES *via* PRESEAU. Next day on again to LE TRIEZ, where billets were secured with difficulty. The roads *en route* were simply awful, and progress was slow and difficult owing largely to the continual stream of traffic.

On the morning of the 6th November the Infantry continued their advance and our men were used in small patrols ahead of the Infantry, after objectives were gained, to ascertain enemy positions. The BOIS de DANDOIS was reconnoitred (E. of AUTREPPE and our own dispositions, as well as those of the enemy, marked and reported to Brigadier, who sent for the Company Commander and thanked him for the clear and useful reports.

On the 7th moved to ROISIN, and next day to vicinity of BOIS d'ANGRE where patrols were sent out to locate enemy who was found at EUGNIES and engaged, the Infantry (9th South Staffs) then advanced and relieved our patrols.

On the 9th the Company moved to AULNOIS, and being the first troops in this village received a great reception from the inhabitants.

On the 10th moved on to QUEVY LE GRAND and patrols were sent out in direction of IHY and S. of HARVENGT to ascertan positions of enemy and gain possession of high ground in that vicinity. This was accomplished with very little opposition, and on Infantry arriving our patrols returned to QUEVY LE GRAND.

Next morning, the 11th, news was received at 10.0 a.m. hat hostilities were to cease at 11.0 a.m. and that the Company was transferred from 11th Division to 63rd (R.N.) Division.

The G.O.C. 33rd Brigade (11th Division) sent to the Company Commander (T. Capt. H. C. Knubley, M.C.) a letter of appreciation of the consistent good services given by all ranks.

Next day the Company rejoined the Battalion at AULNOIS.

Battalion Headquarters remained at RAMILLIES and carried on its administrative duties to Companies from there until the 3rd November, when orders to move forward were received. The destination was HASPRES which was reached by noon. No. 2 Company was in that village and they with No. 3 were sent on to ARTRES that afternoon.

The Battalion Headquarters only stayed the night in HASPRES and next morning marched out with QUERENAING for destination. Arrived at 11.0 a.m. and there received orders from 11th Division (to whom we were attached) to go on to PRESEAU, which village was reached at 4.0 p.m. and billets secured with difficulty as the village was very badly damaged and there was hardly a sound house left. However, with our customary luck, we managed to get fairly good quarters.

The roads from HASPRES were in bad order—the enemy did not keep his roads in nearly as good order as we did—and the traffic was tremendous—lorries, wagons, guns, cars, etc., and made a continuous stream for the whole of the way from HASPRES.

Narrative of No. 3 Company

The inhabitants of Valenciennes, wishing to mark the occasion of the release of the town from German domination, invited the Army Commander to receive an address in company with representatives of all troops concerned in the capture. Accordingly, on the 8th November, representatives of the Army assembled at the Grand Place and an address was presented to Sir H. Horne. H.R.H. the Prince of Wales was present. This unit was represented by one officer and twelve other ranks.

At PRESEAU Battalion Headquarters remained for several days and on the 9th November moved on to ROISIN, where it only stayed for the night, trekking further forward to AULNOIS next day, where good quarters were secured, and it was in this village that we were when the news of the Armistice being signed reached us.

The day following all the three Companies which had been out with Divisions rejoined, and were accommodated in a large unfinished factory.

At 11.0 o'clock on the 11th November, 1918, when hostilities were suspended, the Battalion was distributed as follows :—

Battalion Headquarters at AULNOIS attached 11th Division.

No. 1 Company (Captain H. D. McHugh. M.C.) at ATHIS attached 56th Division.

No. 2 Company (T. Capt. Blomfield, M.C.) at GIRVY attached 63rd (R.N.) Division.

No. 3 Company (T. Capt. Knubley, M.C.) at QUEVY LE GRAND attached 11th Division.

The Corps occupied a front extending from half-a-mile W. of ESTINNE au MONT northwards to a point about a mile north of VILLERS-SAINT-CHICLAIN, and this line formed the outpost line at the Armistice hour.

The news of the signing of the Armistice and cessation of hostilities was received with great joy by all ranks. The thought that our object after fighting for over four years, had been gained, and our enemy, the enemy of all civilization, had been forced to his knees, gave a sense of great relief to us all, and the joy of every soldier and the inhabitants of the village was manifested by cheering, flag waving, music, etc. AULNOIS Village hailed our men as its saviours because our No. 3 Company was the first of the British troops to enter in pursuit of the flying enemy a few days earlier, and our boys got a great reception.

The operations of the various Companies of the Battalion throughout the advances from CAMBRAI to MONS during the period 10th October to 11th November were carried out under unfavourable conditions of weather and roads, long hours and marches, indifferent billets, often short rations, but the unfailing energy and resource of all ranks, characteristic of our army, prevailed, and never once was a job, however difficult and trying, left undone or half done. Each successive Divisional or Brigade General we were under (and we served 5 Divisions during the advance) expressed himself very pleased with the troops. To the N.C.O.'s and men concerned in the supply of rations a special mention is due—their work entailed long journeys at all hours over bad roads, frequently shelled, and their devotion to their duty earned for them the hearty thanks of all ranks.

As a reward for the work done the following decorations were awarded :—

MILITARY CROSS :

BAR TO MILITARY MEDAL.

Sergt.	F. A. Sutherland, M.M.
Corpl.	S. C. Forrester, M.M.
Private	H. Gallagher, M.M.

MILITARY MEDAL.

Lance Corpl.	J. Wharton
Private	D. T. McMeeking
Sergeant	L. F Lees
Sergeant	W. G. Brown, D.C.M.
Sergeant	C. E. H. Dass
Corporal	C. D. Matthews
Sergeant	C. E. Hounsell
Corporal	G. McGregor

Chapter XX.

THE ARMISTICE.

The Corps Commander (Lieut. General Sir Alexander J. Godley, K.C.B., K.C.M.G.), issued a special order appreciative of the work done by the Corps, of which the following is a copy :—

SPECIAL ORDER.

by

Lieut.Gen. Sir A. J. Godley, K.C.B., K.C.M.G.
Commanding XXII. Corps.

I desire on the concluson of the Armistice with the enemy to-day to thank all ranks of the Corps for the gallantry and devotion to duty which they have displayed, and to express my admiration of their conduct. The manner in which the troops after the great exertion of the previous years and the desperate defensive battles of this spring, responded to the call for a renewed offensive, has no equal in history.

I am fully sensible to the strain imposed on Units, often depleted in numbers by the maintenance of the constant pressure which has finally worn out the enemy's power of resistance.

It was not superiority in numbers but superiority in dogged determination and courage which, in spite of the physical obstacle of successive river lines, and in spite of the difficulties created by the enemy and the hardships imposed by bad weather, broke down the enemy's defence.

Commanders and Staffs, R.A.F., Corps Mounted Troops, Artillery, Engineers, Infantry, Machine Gunners, Labour Units, Transport, R.A.M.C., Ordnance Services and Veterinary Services have worked loyally together toward the same end, and I congratulate them on their share in the victory of which they may all justly be proud.

     (Sgd.)   ALEX. J. GODLEY,
            Lieut.-General
         Commanding XXII. Corps.

Headquarters,
 XXII. Corps, 11th November, 1918.

 The concentration of the Battalion at AULNOIS was complete by evening of 12th November, and all ranks settled down for a rest and refitting. On 15th November 8 officers and 100 other ranks went to MONS and there took part in the official entry by the Army Commander, General Sir H. Horne, into the city, which was a fine show, some 10,000 troops taking part.

 Training, principally of a recreational nature, was carried on for remainder of the month.

 On 29th, intimation was received that the Australian personnel of the Corps Mounted Troops was leaving the Corps to join the Australian Corps, and Lieut.-Colonel S. G. Hindhaugh, D.S.O., who had commanded for the past two years, visited the Battalion to say farewell. A parade was held and the Colonel made some very complimentary remarks and expressed his regret at the severance of his connection with the New Zealand personnel.

 Since the Armistice was signed various rumours had been circulating regarding our inclusion in the Armies of Occupation in Germany, and opinions were divided to whether we would go or not. However, on 30th November, doubts were set at rest by orders being received that the Battalion would move to BAUDOUR about 16 miles in a northerly direction and billet there for the winter.

Accordingly we packed up and moved, arriving at midday. The billeting party had secured us fine accommodation—Nos. 1 and 3 Companies in a fine large chateau, and No. 2 in the Gendarmerie, Headquarters being accommodated in houses. Here the Unit soon made itself comfortable, and finding the inhabitants kind and hospitable, all ranks soon had friends. The war being over, military training was not carried out to much extent, only sufficient to keep everybody fit. Sports Committees were formed and arrangements for education under our Padre, L. A. Knight, and 2nd Lieut. C. C. Southey, M.C., M.M., were made, and their classes were well attended. Football (our National winter game) was played frequently. Teams from each Company and Headquarters played a tournament which was eventually won by Battalion Headquarters **Team.** Several outside matches were arranged with

156 Battery, R.F.A.
South African Heavy Artillery
New Zealand Railway Engineers
and others, with varying results.

The Corps Rugby Championship was fought out between our team and O.M.R. combined, and the S.A.H.A. at Mons; the South Africans won, but were given a good go for it. (5 to 3).

A rifle range was built and Rifle and Revolver Matches were held.

The O.M.R. Squadron was with us all this time, and with this Unit formed the XXII. Corps Mounted Troops under command of Lieut.-Colonel C. Hellier Evans, D.S.O. Captain H. D. McHugh, M.C., was promoted to Field rank as 2nd in command of the Battalion, and Lieuts. C. G. Johnson (Q.M.), A. C. P. Hay and D. G. Cody were promoted to Captain.

Up to the end of November the M.O. of Corps Mounted Troops attended our Medical wants. On

The Armistice

departure of Australian personnel, Captain F. Dewsbury Penfold, N.Z.M.C., was attached to the Battalion and O.M.R. as Medical Officer.

At end of December all the officers and men of 1914 and 1915 classes were sent to England for demobilization and from this Unit one officer (2nd Lieut. D. H. Evans) and 23 other ranks were sent.

Leave to U.K., and places in France and Belgium was liberal, and many took advantage of the privilege ; those going to U.K. were mostly retained for demobilization.

The historic field of Waterloo was within easy distance and lorry excursions were arranged, as were trips to Brussels, Lille and other towns.

Concerts, dances and cinema entertainments were held in the "Salon d'Harmonie" at frequent intervals. The Battalion Pierrots under 2nd Lieut. W. E. Randall, D.C.M., provided several very enjoyable concerts. The Pierrot Troupe consisted of 2nd Lieut. Randall, conductor, Corpl. P. R. Boagey, pianist, Corpl. C. D. Matthews, Privates C. Wright, J. D. Donaldson, B. J. O'Connell, J. Connell and C. R. Foster.

The cessation of hostilities in November, 1918, brought permission from G.H.Q. for the use of cameras again, these having been prohibited during the war, and so it became possible to indulge in this mild form of amusement, but the opportunity of securing really interesting photos of war scenes was gone, and only those scenes of a more or less peace-time period were obtainable ; still those with an inclination that way used up quite a lot of films, and some useful snaps resulted.

The winter spent at BAUDOUR was a very cold one and snow fell frequently, and for weeks everything was under a mantle of snow. Our quarters, however, were comfortable, fuel was p entiful, and so no great inconvenience was experienced.

Early in January our Corps Commander, Lieut. General Sir A. J. Godley, K.C.B., K.C.M.G., who has always taken an interest in his cyclists, visited us and presented the decorations awarded to its officers and other ranks during the six months preceding the Armistice. The Battalion was paraded in front of the Chateau and the General presented each in turn with a ribbon of the decoration, making a splendid speech at the conclusion.

BATTALION PIERROT TROUPE.

THE CHATEAU BAUDOUR.
Our Last Billet in Belgium.

CHAPTER XXI.

OUR DEPARTURE FROM FRANCE.

After spending over three months at BAUDOUR orders were received that the Unit would shortly leave for U.K. preparatory for embarkation to New Zealand for demoblization, and on 18th March, the cycles, wagons and all regimental stores having been previously moved into Mons and stored, the Unit bade good-bye to BAUDOUR and moved by motor lorries to Mons, and from there entrained to ROUEN, from whence after a brief stay it crossed to England and there ceased to exist as a Unit, each officer and man being drafted to his Demobilisation Group.

Major H. D. McHugh, M.C., Captain C. C. Johnson, the Q.M. and 20 others remained at Mons to guard the stores until same could be railed to Calais and be handed over to the Ordnance Department. This was not done for about six weeks owing to the congestion on the French and Belgian lines.

Before the Battalion left Belgium the Corps Commander sent the following letter to our C.O. :—

"In view of the probable early demobilisation of the New Zealand Cyclist Battalion, I desire to place on record my high appreciation of the good service done since the formation of the Battalion in July, 1916, to the signing of the Armistice.

" Your Battalion has had a most varied experience and few Units in the B.E.F. have rendered valuable service in so many different directions or in conjunction with so many different formations.

" Its work has included traffic control, the felling of trees, cable burying, repairing of trenches, the holding as Infantry of Sections of the front line, the reconnaissance of front areas and the participation in offensives as advanced mounted troops.

"The work of burying cables 6, 7, and 8 feet deep, running up to the front line in shell-swept areas, and most of it done by night, proved as valuable and successful as it was arduous and dangerous. Latterly the Battalion became so experienced and expert in this work that its personnel were employed only as supervisors.

"On several occasions when specially needed, your Battalion has done most valuable service in the front line both as Infantry and Mounted Troops. Of these I desire to specially mention the Battle of Messines, the filling of the gap near VIERSTRATT at a heavy cost in casualties, and the holding off of the enemy for four days in April, 1918, during the critical period of the big enemy offensive; the capture of MARFAUX in the offensive of the Fifth French Army in July, 1918, and the excellent patrol and advanced reconnaissance work in the second Battle of the SOMME, and finally in our final advance from Arras to Mons.

"I congratulate you on being selected as the only British Unit to receive a fanion from General Berthelot.

"If Cyclists are included in the post war Army of New Zealand, the traditions of your good service cannot fail to permanently stimulate both their efficiency and *esprit de corps*.

"I ask you with confidence to continue until discharged in New Zealand to do your share in maintaining the high reputation for soldierly qualities held by the N.Z.E.F.

"My gratitude for your services, and my best wishes for your future happiness and prosperity, will follow you to New Zealand.

"Will you please bring the contents of this letter to notice of ranks under your command.

(Sgd.) "ALEX. J. GODLEY,
Lieut.-General
Commanding N.Z. Expeditionary Forces.

6th March, 1919."

PARADE FOR DEMOBILIZATION, FEBY. 1919.

WAITING FOR H.M. THE KING.

Our Departure from France

Such an appreciation as the foregoing cannot but make everyone who served in the Unit feel proud, and its receipt gave the greatest satisfaction to everyone, particularly those who had been Cyclists since the Unit's formation.

In addition to the letter our General visited and inspected the Unit at Mons Railway Station before it entrained, and in a brief address thanked all ranks for the very creditable work done during the past three years.

The cadre, consisting of a selected party from the Otago Mounted Rifles and another from the Cyclists, under Major H. D. McHugh, M.C., received orders on the 4th May to load the Unit's equipment on railway trucks at Mons and proceed to Calais, where it was to be handed over.

We left Mons on May 5th, and three day's journey brought us to Calais, where the equipment was handed over to the Ordnance Department and the necessary receipts obtained. The party left France for England on the 10th of May, and on arrival in London were given the usual 14 days' leave, after which they were absorbed into the Demobilisation Units at our bases, Sling and Codford.

Chapter XXII.

PRESENTATION OF FANION, EPERNAY.

It will be remembered that the Battalion was in July and August, 1918, with the Corps in the Champagne District, where it gained considerable glory for its work whilst associated with the Fifth French Army under General A. Berthelot.

The Maire and Municipality of the the town of EPERNAY (Department of the Marne) wishing to signalise the victory of the Second Battle of the Marne which, by turning the enemy back when within a few kilometers of the town saved Epernay and adjoining towns from devastation from the enemy, presented through General Berthelot to our Corps and several of the French units who were in action at that time, fanions or banners to commemorate the victory. Our Corps Commander nominated our Battalion to receive the honour, his selection being made from all the British Battalions engaged.

This was a very high compliment to us, and gave the greatest satisfaction to all.

The presentation of the fanion was fixed to take place at Epernay on the 20th July, 1919, the anniversary of the opening of the Second Battle of the Marne, and the C.O. was invited by the Maire to visit Epernay with a delegation to receive the presentation.

As the Unit was disbanded and most of the officers and men had already left for New Zealand, it was not easy to secure a party. Eventually, after one postponement, a small party consisting of three officers and nine other ranks left London for Epernay, *via* Paris, arriving there a day or so before the eventful day, which was fixed for Sunday, 27th July, 1919.

PRESENTATION OF FANION, EPERNAY 113

The town, the home of the champagne manufacture, was *en fête* for the occasion, and representatives of ten French Units and one Italian Unit, which had also participated in the operations of the Second Battle of the Marne, were present to receive fanions allotted to them.

Our Unit was represented by :—

Lieut. Col.	C. Hellier Evans, D.S.O.
Captain	T. H. Dickinson, Adjutant
Captain	C. G. Johnson, Quartermaster
R S.M.	A. Turner
Q.M.S	E. F. Bisney
Sergeant	Tasker
Sergeant	Paget
Corporal	T. Taylor
Private	Pemberton
Private	May
Private	Winkie
Private	Storm

whilst Captain G. L. Comer, Lieut. N. P. Branson, and Lieut. C. C. Southey, M.C., M.M., were with the parties as visitors.

The ceremonies started on the Saturday night by a torchlight procession and military tattoo by the 54th French Infantry Regiment. On Sunday morning the lengthy programme started by the reception of M. Nail, Minister of Justice and General A. Berthelot, who arrived rom Paris. The Maire was visited and welcoming speeches were made, then followed the visit to the military cemetery. The principal event, the presentation of the fanion, took place in the Square at 11 a.m. before a large crowd, the recipients forming a hollow square in front of a dias erected for the purpose. Several speeches were made by Dignitaries and at their conclusion the Maire of Epernay presented the banners ; our Unit was first, and as Captain Dickinson stepped forward to receive it, the cheers of the assembled multitude testified to the popularity of our troops and the town's gratitude to us for our share in freeing it from the danger of the enemy. The other presentations followed, first the Italian Delegation and then the ten French Units, all of which were accorded hearty applause. More speeches followed, and then the troops marched through the streets, our party leading the procession. The Military and Civil Dignataries, with all the visiting officers then adjourned to the Maire, where a splended lunch was provided, and some very congratulatory speeches were made ; the Maire's reference to our Army was most cordially received.

The next day (Monday) the group was photographed and afterwards left for Paris where the night was spent, the journey to England *via* Boulogne being continued next day.

Whilst at Epernay facilities were given us by the French Authorities to visit the scenes of our Battle at Marfaux, over a year previous. All the party visited the battlefield, and those who had been in the scrap found satisfaction in living again the stirring times. The graves of those who fell were visited also.

M. Le Comte de Chandon-Moét, the principal of the great firm of champagne makers (Moét and Chandon) was particularly kind to us. He entertained the officers at his house and did all he could to make our stay enjoyable. The N.C.O.'s and men were the guests of the French Red Cross, and were very well looked after.

Everyone of the party thoroughly enjoyed the trip— it formed a very fine break in the monotony of life, and all carry with them the most cordial recollections of the kindness and hospitality of our Gallant French Allies.

The fanion has been greatly admired by all who have seen it, and many congratulations have been received by the Unit on being the only N.Z. Unit to have such a high honour conferred on it.

Presentation of Fanion, Epernay

So ends the history of the Cyclists' part in the Great War which engaged the close attention of all British subjects during the years of 1914 to 1918.

The majority of members have returned to New Zealand, a few taking their discharges in England, and settling in other parts of the world.

Of our Battalion 59 of our lads have been left behind on the Glorious Battlefields of France where they fell. The inspiration given by the deeds of these brave lads did not end with their lives, but is passed on to build up the soul of our Empire, and furthermore we lay, as it were, a wreath upon their graves.

We take this opportunity of congratulating the majority of our lads on their safe return to the Homeland, and may they prosper.

With undaunted spirit they went forth to give all they had to give, and we crown them with laurel for their efforts in the Great Cause of the Empire.

It is sure to say that our lads have gained materially by their War experience, besides receiving an education generally from the peoples on the other side of the world, and all are proud to have formed a part in that Great Army which rid the world of a Prussian menace.

NEW ZEALAND CYCLIST BATTALION.

STATISTICS.

STRENGTH :

	Officers	Other Ranks	Total
The original Cyclist Company	6	*211	217
Reinforcements	16	475	491
			708

*Ten of the original Company were susbequently commissioned.

The above figures do not include 6 Officers and 200 other ranks, Australian Personnel, with 2nd Anzac Cyclist Battalion from 21/7/16 to 16/1/18.

	Officers	Other Ranks	Total
Killed in action, N.Z. Personnel only	4	55	59
Wounded. *	7	252	259

*Fifty-one of these were wounded more than once.

Number with Unit at Armistice, 11/11/18.
    8 Officers, 286 other ranks.

BILLETS.

During service in France and Belgium from 18/7/16 to 18/3/19, equalling 2 years and 8 months, the Unit occupied 82 different Billets and Bivouacs.

Three of these absorbed 11 months of the period, therefore for the balance of the time the Unit moved its location on an average about once a week.

THE FANION PRESENTATION PARTY.

A CAPTURED GERMAN CYCLE.

APPENDIX 117

ROLL OF HONOUR of Officers, N.C.O.'s and Men killed in action or died of wounds.

No.	Rank	Name	Date of Casualty	Place
10716	Lieut.	J. T. Steven	17/11/17	Westhoek, near Ypres
24/2128	Lieut.	C. A. Dickeson, M.C.	26/4/18	Hallebast, Corner, Vierstraat
11583	2nd Lieut.	D. C. Griffith	23/7/18	Marfaux
32540	2nd Lieut.	A. E. M. Rowland	23/7/18	Marfaux
10747	Cpl.	C. S. DesBarres	30/9/16	Laventie
10820	Private	A. F. George	1/11/16	Armentieres
10866	Private	T. P. Milne	8/11/16	Armentieres
10795	Private	A. L. M. Duff	7/6/17	Messines
10773	Private	— Cavins	7/6/17	Messines
11/2226	Private	D. J. Shewry	7/6/17	Messines
10296	Private	C. Barwick	11/6/17	Messines
10754	Private	C. L. Anstey	12/6/17	Messines
10883	Private	M. A. Pankhurst	10/7/17	Ploegsteert
10845	Private	A. P. Kay	10/7/17	Ploegsteert
16007	Private	A. Stokes	22/12/17	Westhoek, Ypres
17090	Private	P. Mudie	3/1/18	Vlamertinghe
9/366	Private	J. S. Clarke	25/3/18	Yyres
26/1099	Private	W. Potter	30/3/18	Shrewsbury Forest, Zillebeke
27160	Private	W. Burrows	16/4/18	Kemmel (Mount)
5/29	Private	V. E. Hodson	16/4/18	Kemmel (Mount)
24485	Private	W. E. J. Browne	17/4/18	Memmel (Mount)
10837	Private	A. W. Hunter	17/4/18	Kemmel (Mount)
10887	Private	T. E. Power	18/4/18	Kemmel (Mount)
10783	Private	T. J. Clinton	18/4/18	Kemmel (Mount)
10827	Private	R. E. Harris	23/4/18	Hallebast Corner, Vierstraat
10749	Sergeant (T./C.S.M.	T. C. Hodgson	23/4/18	Kemmel (Mount)
25/624	Private	O. Fisher	25/4/18	Vierstraat
25/1126	Private	A. Gold	25/4/18	Vierstraat
10930	Private	J. D. Welsh	26/4/18	Hallebast Corner, Vierstraat
20110	Private	R. H. Curtis	27/4/18	Hallebast Corner, Vierstraat
24/1864	Private	H. R. Williams	27/4/18/	Hallebast Corner, Vierstraat
24/2043	Private	D. Mulcahy	29/4/18	Hallebast Corner, Vierstraat

No.	Rank	Name	Date of Casualty	Place
10813	Sergeant	H. Gilchrist, M.M.	6/5/18	Vierstraat
17894	Private	L. L. Martin	5/7/18	Kemmel (Mount)
45181	Private	F. Baker	23/7/18	Marfaux
10779	Private	R. A. Chatwin	23/7/18	Marfaux
10807	L/Sergt.	O. R. Foulds	23/7/18	Marfaux
10819	L/Corpl.	G. Grindrod	23/7/18	Marfaux
59654	Private	H. J. Johnson	23/7/18	Marfaux
10851	Private	A. R. Kloth	23/7/18	Marfaux
13/3129	Private	H. J. Lindsay	23/7/18	Marfaux
10731	Sergeant	H. Matthews, M.M.	23/7/18	Marfaux
10047	Private	A. J. McLaughlin	23/7/18	Marfaux
51865	Private	A. R. McLeod	23/7/18	Marfaux
28511	Private	H. Mills	23/7/18	Marfaux
18891	Private	L. A. Newman	23/7/18	Marfaux
18891	Private	L. A. Newman	23/7/18	Marfaux
25/456	Private	A. J. Perry	23/7/18	Marfaux
13120	Private	A. E. Smith	23/7/18	Marfaux
46397	Private	F. W. T. Smith	23/7/18	Marfaux
10928	Private	R. H. Turner	23/7/18	Marfaux
102763	Private	F. A. A. Simmiss	24/7/18	Marfaux
102629	Private	F. Hannam	29/7/18	Marfaux
16214	L/Corpl.	R. A. Foote	4/8/18/	Marfaux
10/4008	Private	J. T. Thacker	30/8/18	Aulnois
28211	Private	R. H. Read	27/9/18/	Near Arras
13533	Private	J. F. Spear	1/11/18/	Aulnois
46504	Private	R. D. Walker	1/11/18	Saultain
10370	Sergeant	H. L. Midgley, M.M.	7/11/18	Serbourquiaux
13016	Private	J. F. Harston	10/11/18	Quevy Le Grand

SUMMARY.

Officers	4
N.C.O.'s	8
Men	47
	59

APPENDIX

HONOURS LIST.

Distinguished Service Order.

No.	Rank	Name	Date	Action
10711	Lt. Col.	C. Hellier Evans	June, 1917	Messines

Bar to Military Cross.

25/4	Major	H. D. McHugh, M.C.	June, 1919	Cambrai, Mons Advance, 1918

Military Cross.

25/4	Capt.	H. D. McHugh (Now Major)	June, 1917	Messines
24/2128	Lieut.	C. A. Dickeson (A./Capt.) (Killed in action)	Sept./Oct., 1917	Passchendale
10743	Lieut.	H. C. J. Knubley		
4/150A	Lieut.	E. H. Bloomfield	23rd July, 1918	Marfaux, S.W. of Rheims
25/651	2/Lieut.	W. H. Yorke		
10723	2/Lieut.	F. L. Bowron	Sept., 1918	Somme
22438	Lieut.	H. A. Highet		
28617	Lieut.	D. G. Cody	Oct./Nov., 1918	Cambrai-Mons Advance
10918	2/Lieut.	C. C. Southey		
10724	2/Lieut.	L. H. Browne		

Distinguished Conduct Medal.

24844	C.S.M.	G. B. Baker, M.M.	23rd July, 1918	Marfaux
12/324	Private	W. G. Cavenett	Sept., 1918	Somme

Bar to Military Medal.

13502	C.S.M.	R. H. Sly, M.M.	June, 1917	Ploegsteest
10944	S/Sgt.	H. M. Carr, M.M.	Sept., 1918	Somme
23/1206	Sgt.	F. A. Sutherland, M.M.	Sept., 1918	Somme
12700	Cpl.	S. C. Forrester, M.M.	Sept., 1918	Somme
28126	Private	H. Gallagher, M.M.	Sept., 1918	Somme

The Military Medal.

1740	Sergt. (now 2/Lt.)	A. H. Coe	June, 1917	Messines
10899	Private	H. J. Ringham	June, 1917	Messines
3/1722	Private	F. J. Sharpe	June, 1917	Messines
13502	C.S.M.	R. H. Sly	June, 1917	Messines
10758	Cpl.	H. Bellamy	June, 1917	Ploegsteest
24844	C.S.M.	G. B. Baker, D.C.M.	Oct., 1917	Passchendale
10918	Sergt. (now 2/Lt.)	C. C. Southey	Oct., 1917	Passchendale

The Military Medal.

No.	Rank	Name	Date	Action
16465	L./Sergt.	W. I. N. Bond	April, 1918	Mont Kemmell
10/1700	Cpl.	W. H. Whiting	April, 1918	Mont Kemmell
10813	Sergt.	H. Gilchrist (Since died of wounds)	April, 1918	Meteren Strazeele
28126	Private	H. Gallagher		
36966	Private	M. C. Gallagher		
6/690	Private	C. McLean		
6/697	Private	T. Nimmo		
10931	Private	I G. West.		
10/322	Private	A. A. Close		
10731	Sergt.	F. C. Matthews (Since killed in action)	April/May, 1918	Vierstraat
12700	Cpl.	S. C. Forrester		
10944	Sergt.	H. M. Carr		
10739	Private	C. Brown		
10925	C.S.M.	N. H. Thomas		
10784	Sergt.	H. E. Coats		
23/1206	Sergt.	F. A. Sutherland	23rd July, 1918	Marfaux
10912	Private	J. E. Shewry		
3/1381	Private	A. J. Byron		
14840	Private	A. McCullagh		
24946	Cpl.	I. W. Weston		
10768	Sergt.	F. E. Brown		
20952	Private	F. Barlow	Sept., 1918	Somme
10945	Sergt.	R. Ryan		
10370	Sergt.	H. L. Midgley (Since died of wounds)		
10932	L/Cpl.	J. Warton		
10875	Private	D. J. McMeeking		
10852	Sergt.	T. F. Lees		
12/3569	Sergt.	W. G. Brown, D.C.M.	Oct./Nov., 1918	Cambrai-Mons Advance
10168	Sergt.	C. E. H. Daas		
22632	Cpl.	F. D. Matthews		
21686	Sergt.	G. E. Hounsell		
10873	Cpl.	G. McGregor		

Meritorious Service Medal.

No.	Rank	Name	Date	Action
10869	Sgnl Sgt	G. B. Morton	Oct., 191	Passchendale, Operation
10741	R.Q.M.S.E.	G. D. Eden		
10901	S/Sergt.	L. E. Rowley	Feb./Dec., 1918	Operations Western Front
10787	Private	C. E. Cragg		

APPENDIX

Foreign Decorations (French).
Chevalier de la Legion D'Honneur.

Liet. Col.C. Hellier Evans, D.S.O. July, 1918 Marfaux

La Medaille Militaire.

No.	Rank	Name	Date	Action
10745	R.S.M.	A. Turner		
9/1466	Private	A. McIntosh	July, 1918	Marfaux
	C.S.M.	Henderson		
	Cpl.	Hurley		

La Croix De Guerre.

| 12/1682 | Sergt. | W. Jamieson | July, 1918 | Marfaux |
| 14844 | Private | C. D. McLaren | | |

La Croix De Guerre (Belgian).

| 10925 | C.S.M. | N. H. Thomas, M.M. | | |
| 10807 | L/Sergt. | G. R. Foulds | Oct. 1917 | Passchendale |

(Since killed in action)

Chevalier Crown of Roumania (Roumanian).

Lieut. (T./Capt.) T. H. Dickinson 30/12/18 Operations Western Front

Mentions in Despatches, 8.

Good Service Certificates,. 12.

SUMMARY

Decorations.

British.			French.	Foreign.
D.S.O.	..	1	Legion d'Honneur	1
Bar to M.C.	..	1	Medaille Militaire	4
M.C.	..	10	Crox de Geurre..	2
D.C.M.	..	2	**Belgian**—Crox de Guerre	2
Bar to M.M.	..	5	**Roumanian.**—Crown of	
M.M.	..	39	Roumania	1
M.S.M.	..	4		

122 NEW ZEALAND CYCLIST CORPS

Nominal Roll of Original Personnel of New Zealand Cyclist Corps who embarked from New Zealand on 5th May, 1916.

10911	Major	Evans, C. H. D.	W
10716	2nd Lieutenant	Steven, J. T.	K
10713	2nd Lieutenant	Comer, G. L.	
10714	2nd Lieutenant	Johnson, C. G. G.	
10712	2nd Lieutenant	Clark-Walker, G.	
10715	2nd Lieutenant	Kebbell, R. W.	
10748	L.-Corporal	Agnew, G.	
10752	Private	Edenbrooke, J. K.	
10754	Private	Anstey, C. L.	D W
10755	Private	Ashworth, S. H.	W
10756	Private	August, C.	
10753	Private	Angove, A.	W
10717	Q.M.-Sergeant	Bisney, E. F.	
10723	Sergeant	Bowron, F. L.	
10724	Sergeant	Browne, L. H.	
10940	Corporal	Banks, J.	
10738	Corporal	Betchley, F. F.	
10739	Corporal	Brown, C.	W
10757	Private	Barker, A. B.	
10758	Private	Bellamy, H.	W
10759	Private	Billman, V.	W
10760	Private	Blair, A. T.	2 W
10761	Private	Boagey, P. R.	
10762	Private.	Bolt, H. S.	
10763	Private	Bowers, H. D. W.	
10765	Private	Branson, N. P.	W
10766	Private	Bravo, V. S.	
10768	Private	Brown, F. E.	
10769	Private	Bruce, G. F.	W
10770	Private	Burns, T. D.	2 W
10771	Private	Butler, E. G.	W
10942	Private	Barrett, W. W.	
10296	Private	Barwick, O.	D W
10767	Private	Broughan, A. F.	
10740	Corporal	Coe, A. H.	
10775	Private	Cantwell, R. H.	W
10776	Private	Carlyon, E. J.	
10777	Private	Carrie, J. G.	
10778	Private	Charleston, J. C. R.	W
10779	Private	Chatwin, R. A.	K

W denotes Wounded   D W denotes Died of Wounds
2 W denotes Twice Wounded   D S denotes Died of Sickness
K denotes Killed in Action

APPENDIX

10781	Private	Clark, F. D.	W
10782	Private	Claydon, F. F.	
10783	Private	Clinton, T. J.	K
10784	Private	Coats, H. E.	W
10785	Private	Corkhill, H.	W
10786	Private	Crabb, L. J.	2 W
10787	Private	Cragg, E. C.	
10944	Private	Carr, H. M.	
10788	Private	Cuningham, S. A.	W
10789	Private	Curgenven, W. L.	
10791	Private	Christie, G.	W
10943	Private	Cameron, L. G.	W
10949	Private	Cumming, F. G.	W
10772	Private	Cabot, J. T.	
10774	Private	Cameron, R. S.	
10725	L.-Sergeant	Dickinson, T. H.	
10747	Corporal	Des Barres, C. S.	K
10793	Private	Dickey, N. R.	
10794	Private	Dobson, G.	2 W
10795	Private	Duff, A. L. M.	K
10796	Private	Duncan, R. D.	W
10741	Corporal	Eden, E. G. D.	
10797	Private	Ensor, R. W.	W
10798	Private	Edwards, P. F.	W
10799	Private	Emmett, J.	W
10800	Private	Evans, R. R.	
10727	Sergeant	Fox, E. G.	
10803	Private	Finlay, R. W.	W
10802	Private	Findlay, F. A.	
10805	Private	Fitzmaurice, W.	
10806	Private	Foster, C. R.	
10807	Private	Foulds, G. R.	K
10808	Private	Fraser, H.	2 W
10810	Private	Fuller, A. E.	
12700	Private	Forrester, S. C.	
10811	Private	Geddes, J.	W
10812	Private	Gibson, H. J.	
10813	Private	Gilchrist, H.	D W
10814	Private	Gourley, S. C.	
10815	Private	Grant, A.	
10816	Private	Gray, G. F.	W
10818	Private	Greenslade, S.	

W denotes Wounded   D W denotes Died of Wounds
2 W denotes Twice Wounded   D S denotes Died of Sickness
K denotes Killed in Action

10819	Private	Grindrod, C.	K
10820	Private	George, A. F.	K
10821	Private	Garrett, W. J.	
10721	C.S.M.	Hay, A. C. P.	W
10746	Corporal	Hart, E. G. L.	
10749	L.-Corporal	Hodgson, T. C.	D W
10751	L.-Corporal	Hill, J. S.	W
10822	Private	Haigh, W. E.	W
10823	Private	Hall, R. C.	
10824	Private	Hanna, T. R.	W
10825	Private	Hansen, G.	W
10826	Private	Hardy, C. J.	
10827	Private	Harris, R. E.	D W
10828	Private	Harvey, C. N.	W
10829	Private	Hebden, F.	W
10831	Private	Hill, F. H.	
10832	Private	Hobbs, C. V.	D S
10833	Private	Holmes, F. W. H.	
10834	Private	Horne, W.	
10838	Private	Hurley, G. A. R.	
10836	Private	Hughes, R. H.	
10837	Private	Hunter, A. W.	K
10948	Private	Henderson, T. W.	
10728	Sergeant	Ivimey, S. S.	W
10839	Private	Ingham, L. F.	
10729	Private	Jones, F. T.	2 W
10840	Private	Jabocsen, W. G.	
10841	Private	Janes, H. W. J.	
10842	Private	Johnson, G. W.	D S
10843	Private	Johnson, O. A.	W
10844	Private	Jonkers, E. J.	W
10354	Private	Johnson, C. N.	
10742	Corporal	Knowles, W.	
10845	Private	Kay, A. P.	K
10847	Private	Kelling, H.	W
10848	Private	Keys, C. E.	
10849	Private	Keys, E. G.	
10850	Private	Kirk, H.	W
10851	Private	Kloth, A. R.	K
10852	Private	Kerr, C. G.	
10743	Corporal	Knubley, H. C. J.	
10854	Private	Loversidge, R.	W

W denotes Wounded   D W denotes Died of Wounds
2 W denotes Twice Wounded   D S denotes Died of Sickness
K denotes Killed in Action

APPENDIX 125

10855	Private	Lucas, J. P.	W
10857	Private	Lees. T. F.	2 W
10731	Sergeant	Matthews, H.	K
10734	Private	Marks, A. C.	
10737	Private	Morrison, A.	K
10858	Private	Mackenzie, A.	
10859	Private	Mann, W.	
10860	Private	Manson, W.	W
10861	Private	Matthews, T. E.	
10862	Private	May, A. J. L.	W
10863	Private	Mears, A.	W
10864	Private	Mercier, L. St. V.	W
10865	Private	Meredith, R. C.	
10866	Private	Milne, T. P.	D W
10867	Private	Mullins, J. F.	
10868	Private	Murray, E. R.	W
10869	Private	Morton, G. B.	
10370	Private	Midgley, H. L.	D W
10835	Private	Mora, H. F.	
10870	Private	McAuliffe, T. J.	2*W
10871	Private	McCann, P.	W
10872	Private	McDougall, J. M.	
10873	Private	McGregor, G.	
10874	Private	McLaughlin, W. L.	
10875	Private	McMeeking, D. T.	
10877	Private	McLean, W. L. C.	W
10941	Private	McEvoy, W. T.	
10736	Sergeant	Nunn, H. T.	
10878	Private	Neal, T. A.	
10879	Private	Nuttall, W. McL.	W
10881	Private	Orme, A. J.	
10882	Private	Palmer, F. H.	W
10883	Private	Pankhurst, M. A.	K
10884	Private	Pearce, W. G.	
10885	Private	Pemberton, T. H. H.	W
10886	Private	Pengelly, G. E.	
10887	Private	Power, T. E.	K
10888	Private	Pragnell, P.	
10889	Private	Prestidge, F. B.	W
10890	Private	Prince, W. H.	
10891	Private	Rae, F.	W
10892	Private	Raine, R. F.	

W denotes Wounded D W denotes Died of Wounds
2 W denotes Twice Wounded D S denotes Died of Sickness
K denotes Killed in Action

10893	Private	Ramsay, M. S.	W
10894	Private	Ritchie, J.	W
10895	Private	Robertson, G.	2 W
10896	Private	Robertson, W.	
10897	Private	Rogers, C. B.	W
10898	Private	Roiall, J.	
10899	Private	Ringham, H. J.	
10901	Private	Rowley, L. E.	
10903	Private	Rusterholtz, P.	
10904	Private	Rutherford, C. D.	
10905	Private	Ryan, W. J.	
10906	Private	Ryan, W.	
10907	Private	Rees, V. H.	
10945	Private	Ryan, R.	W
10750	L.-Corporal	Sutherland, W.	
10908	Private	Scott, J. O.	W
10909	Private	Scott, R. G.	
10910	Private	Shaw, J. E.	
10911	Private	Shearer, J.	
10912	Private	Shewry, J. E.	2 W
10913	Private	Silvester, A. H.	W
11914	Private	Smith, G. H.	W
10915	Private	Smith, H.	
10916	Private	Smith, H. A.	W
10917	Private	Smith, R. A.	
10918	Private	Southey, C. C.	
10919	Private	Spratt, F. C.	W
10920	Private	Stevens, F.	
10921	Private	Stewart, F. H.	W
10922	Private	Stirling, J.	
10923	Private	Sutherland, A.	W
10745	Corporal	Turner, A.	
10924	Private	Tasker, H. C.	2 W
10925	Private	Thomas, N. H.	
10926	Private	Thompson, J.	
10927	Private	Tourell, J. M.	W
10928	Private	Turner, R. H.	K
10946	Private	Withers, R.	W
10929	Private	Walker, H. J.	W
10575	Private	Welsh, J. D.	K
10931	Private	West, I. G.	W
10932	Private	Wharton, J.	W

W denotes Wounded   D W denotes Died of Wounds
2 W denotes Twice Wounded   D S denotes Died of Sickness
K denotes Killed in Action

Appendix

10933	Private	Wilde, C.	W
10934	Private	Wilson, H.	
10935	Private	Wilson, H. A.	
10936	Private	Wratt, R. W. M.	
10937	Private	Wright, A. A. F.	
10938	Private	Wright, P. M.	
10411	Private	Watson, W. G.	
10413	Private	Whitten, J. A.	
10947	Private	Young, J.	

Nominal Roll of Officers and other ranks joining the New Zealand Cyclist Corps as re-inforcements from 21st July, 1916, to 11th November, 1918—Armistice Day.

25/4	Captain	McHugh, H. D.	
9/1392	2nd Lieutenant	Richards, A. H.	W
6/4578	2nd Lieutenant	Garden, R. L.	
24/2128	2nd Lieutenant	Dickenson, Cl A.	K
28617	2nd Lieutenant	Cody, D. G.	
11583	2nd Lieutenant	Griffith, D. C.	K
22438	2nd Lieutenant	Highet, H. A.	
4/150A	2nd Lieutenant	Bloomfield, E. H.	
12328	2nd Lieutenant	Greville, R. H.	W
18583	2nd Lieutenant	Randell, W. E.	W
26/651	2nd Lieutenant	Yorke, W. H.	W
10/3796	2nd Lieutenant	Wylie, L. T.	W
32540	2nd Lieutenant	Rowland, A. E. M.	K
5/583	2nd Lieutenant	Evans, D. H.	
12/817	2nd Lieutenant	Nicholson, E. C. E.	
5/230A	2nd Lieutenant	Ewen, J. F.	W
24839	Private	Adams, C. T.	
24844	Private	Baker, G. B.	W
25188	Private	Bidgood, E.	
24831	Private	Bircham, A. E.	
13660	Private	Browne, S. H.	
24854	Private	Burd, J. M.	
24878	Private	Chamberlain, E.	W
10773	Private	Cairns	K
10726	Private	Ellison, T. H.	W
24851	Private	Forsyth, W.	

W denotes Wounded   D W denotes Died of Wounds
2 W denotes Twice Wounded   D S denotes Died of Sickness
K denotes Killed in Action

NEW ZEALAND CYCLIST CORPS

11646	Private	Gilkes, G.	W
24834	Private	Griffiths, V. E.	W
11652	Private	Guy, A. L.	
25239	Private	Harris, C. B.	W
13018	Private	Hayes, W. A.	W
24832	Private	Howell, T. R.	
25243	Private	Hughes, A. J.	
11945	Private	Mackinson, A. E.	
25308	Private	Phillips, G. H.	
24928	Private	Rossbottom, R. R.	W
10391	Private	Smith, F.	
16007	Private	Stokes, A.	D W
16006	Private	Shaw, J. W.	
24833	Private	Thorburn, S.	
18031	Private	Webber, G. T.	
24837	Private	Webster. W.	
16003	Private	Walker, E. L.	2 W
24946	Private	Weston, I. W.	
12660	Private	While, A. V.	W
23899	Private	Thomas, L. G.	W
13433	Private	McLachlan, G. P.	W
25295	Private	Oberg, J. A.	
13441	Private	Hogg, C. H.	
13447	Private	Jobson, W. B.	W
16014	Private	Vause, A. G. V.	
16149	Private	Alexander, J.	
17876	Private	Barton-Brown, H. G.	
22594	Private	Bicknell, D. W.	W
26243	Private	Booth, W.	
5/874	Private	Bowler, G. W.	2 W
22595	Private	Burch, B. L.	
27160	Private	Burrows, W.	K
16465	Private	Bond, W. M.	2 W
10440	Private	Cheshire, W. G.	
13515	Private	Clark, R.	
16155	Private	Clark, A. E.	
17881	Private	Druce, A.	W
21667	Private	Dunnett, J.	
16481	Private	Davis, W.	
27162	Private	Ferguson, T. S.	W
17887	Private	Garlick, C.	W

W denotes Wounded D W denotes Died of Wounds
2 W denotes Twice Wounded D S denotes Died of Sickness
K denotes Killed in Action

APPENDIX

27165	Private	Grigg, N. C. W.	W
16164	Private	Hanlen, W.	
17894	Private	Martin, L. L.	D W
22596	Private	Maxton. C. W.	W
24920	Private	Newton, J. W.	W
26312	Private	Petterson, H. P. G.	
13502	Private	Sly, L. W.	W
13532	Private	Sorensen, W.	W
13533	Private	Spear, J. F.	2 W D W
4/1641	Private	Twigger, T.	W
21622	Private	Victor, W.	
5/903	Private	Wawman, E.	W
16197	Private	Green, M. J.	
21584	Private	Isherwood, F.	W
26316	Private	Reilly. H. D.	W
11/2226	Private	Shewry, D. J.	D W
16170	Private	King, F. T. L.	W
13746	Private	Fernendez, R. A.	
25/1207	Private	Antunovich, I. M.	
42465	Private	Bryce, W.	
26236	Private	Bate, J.	
10/3302	Private	Buhlman, J.	
29217	Private	Cate, H. C.	
21954	Private	Dashwood, W. J. H.	
6/2128	Private	Foster, A. G.	
10/1523	Private	Hewitt, H. E.	
5/29	Prviate	Hodson, V. E.	K
37825	Private	King, E. F.	W
17090	Private	Mudie, P.	D W
11070	Private	Mercer, J. C.	W
3/1874	Private	Owen, T. E.	W
12/2469	Private	Simons, R. B.	W
10/1700	Private	Whiting, W. H.	W
12/1652	Private	Harding, H. C.	W
24854	Private	Burd, J. M.	
23916	Private	Stemson, Merritt, J.	
15850	Private	Thompson, W. B.	W
56768	Private	Hughes, A. J.	
10/3169	Private	Annan, W. G. F.	
26760	Private	Adams, P.	W
24/1341	Private	Blyde, J. N.	W
12/3569	L.-Corporal	Brown, W. G.	W

W denotes Wounded   D W denotes Died of Wounds
2 W denotes Twice Wounded   D S denotes Died of Sickness
K denotes Killed in Action

27438	Private	Beatty, B.	
28958	Private	Bennett, E.	
20825	Private	Brott, A.	
25/90	Private	Butler, J.	
12972	Private	Best, H. C.	W
22946	Private	Cropley, H.	W
33300	Private	Chappell, C. E.	
12979	Private	Coughlin, J.	
24/732	Private	Darby, E. G.	
45085	Private	Dabinett, G.	
24/1976	Private	Ede, A. J.	W
24/1677	Private	Fitzgerald, R.	
8/2911	Private	Forrester, J.	W
9/1682	Private	Gallagher, D.	
25/1734	Private	Gillispie, J.	
10718	Private	Haig, W.	W
10/2629	Private	Hannam, F.	D W
23/1066	Private	Hardwick, W. R.	W
34067	Private	Harvey, H. C.	
21831	Private	Hawke, A. J.	
12/4193	Private	Holden, A. E.	
28143	Private	Hooper, J. W.	
12/1682	L.-Corporal	Jamieson, W.	
25/770	Private	Kenyon, H.	W
31858	Private	Kilsby, S. V.	
6/1089	Private	Kirk, J. G.	W
10/2994	Corporal	Larkin, E. A.	2 W
6/1923	Private	Mann, J.	
6/2985	Private	McGregor, W.	
13454	Private	Mathews, A. F.	
20185	Private	Maxwell, H.	
26/366	Private	Moroney, M. P.	W
21881	Private	O'Rourke, D. J.	W
34724	Private	Philip, E. H.	2 W
24/659	Private	Perry, L.	
18072	Private	Pitkethley, N.	
29077	Private	Radcliffe, C. E.	
29193	Private	Rountree, H. B.	W
23/1206	Corporal	Sutherland, F. A.	
23/1478	Corporal	Springer, G. C.	W
10/3745	Private	Springer, H. W.	W
10/1984	Private	Simmons, W. C.	

W denotes Wounded   D W denotes Died of Wounds
2 W denotes Twice Wounded   D S denotes Died of Sickness
K denotes Killed in Action

Appendix 131

26/1714	Private	Saies, J.	
13/3078	Private	Sing, A.	
11962	Private	Southwood, J. B.	
12/452	Private	Stonnell, H. H.	
16980	Private	Sabine, T. A.	
26/210	Private	Spicer, L. W.	W
8/3722	Private	Strode, W. E.	
22292	Private	Taylor, T. J. B.	
26/1050	Private	Thomson, J.	
12/3851	Private	Vegar, T.	W
24/1864	Private	Williams, H. B.	D W
12/4188	Private	Wiles, R. A.	
12/2141	Private	Verner, J. E.	
23/1250	Private	Young, L. L.	
14362	Private	Adams, W. R.	
19117	Private	Christian, S. H.	W
5/705A	Private	Curtis, S. A.	W
12/2705	Private	Galvn, C.	W
13/3677	Private	Hewitt, F.	W
20358	Private	Johnson, R.	W
14844	Private	McLaren, C. D.	W
9/1585	Private	Monk, H. E.	W
10/4169	Private	Pederson, N. C. W.	W
8/2706	Private	Reid, F. W.	
9/2133	Corporal	Titteton, C.	W
10/752	Private	West, A.	
10/1102	Private	West, A.	
10/1012	Private	Williams, H.	2 W
11/2383	Private	Williams, J. H.	
9/1466	Private	McIntosh, A.	
40670	Private	Dickeson, C. G.	W
20952	Private	Barlow, F.	
26/657	Private	Barnes, I. S. G.	
25/593	Private	Bennett, H. A.	
22775	Private	Christensen, H. H.	
23/709	Private	Churchhouse, H.	
9/366	Private	Clarke, J. S.	D W
23/2552	Private	Claydon, C.	
25/855	Private	Clements, E. R.	
10/322	Private	Close, A.	W
23362	Private	Edwards, S.	
25/624	Private	Fisher, O.	K

W denotes Wounded   D W denotes Died of Wounds
2 W denotes Twice Wounded   D S denotes Died of Sickness
K denotes Killed in Action

NEW ZEALAND CYCLIST CORPS

10978	Private	Gerard, C.	
13440	Private	Hayes, A. C.	W
28137	Private	Huckle, H.	
12202	Private	Kennedy, J. T.	
25/1775	Private	Levet, C. T.	W
22632	Private	Matthews, C. D.	
23/830	Private	Whitmore, C.	
12226	Private	Monyihan, T.	
24/2043	Private	Mulcahy, D.	K
7/979	Corporal	McAuley, T. H.	
14840	Private	McCullagh, A.	
24/508	L.-Corporal	McNaughton, W. G.	
12242	Private	Newberry, J.	
6/697	Private	Nimmo, T.	
8/4200	Private	Pahi, H.	
26/1099	Private	Potter, W.	D W
6/3837	Private	Prebble, H. F.	W
20246	Private	Seal, H.	
23/2587	Private	Shand, W. L.	W
8/3072	Corporal	Slaughter, R. J.	
13612	Private	Sluce, D.	
13120	Private	Smith, A. E.	K
21617	Private	Stanley, G. A.	W
14342	Private	Watts, T.	
13382	Private	Wilson, D. N. A.	W
14921	Private	Barwell, A. E.	W
10168	L.-Corporal	Dass, C. E. H.	
21686	Private	Hounsell, G. E.	
24193	Private	McDonald, T. W.	W
10047	Private	McLaughlin, A. J.	K
6/690	Private	McLean, C.	
6/4128	Private	Prebble, F. W.	
22459	Private	Skudder, S. B.	W
6/3192	Private	Walker, H. E.	2 W
23/1865	Private	Waters, J.	W
10/1491	Private	Gardner, H.	2 W
10/3310	Private	Jones, C. E.	
23/576	Private	Relph, E. A.	
18868	Private	Stretton, C. W.	
2/1368	Private	Mercer, H. S.	
9/570	Private	Stuart, W.	W
46504	Private	Walker, R. D.	K

W denotes Wounded   D W denotes Died of Wounds
2 W denotes Twice Wounded   D S denotes Died of Sickness
K denotes Killed in Action

Appendix

24270	Private	Boon, W. J.	
24485	Private	Brown, W. E. J.	K
21568	Private	Deary, J.	
12360	Private	Donaldson, E.	
25/538	Private	Ellenberger, D.	D W
12/2696	Private	Fisher, J. H.	
28126	Private	Gallagher, H.	
36966	Private	Gallagher, M. C.	
25/1126	Private	Gold, A.	K
13/2446	Private	Henry, A. W.	W
14648	Private	Larsen, A.	
18891	Private	Newman, L. A.	K
25/456	Private	Perry, A. J.	K
8/3041	Private	Porter, J.	
17/310	Private	Pritchard, J. A.	W
14873	Private	Sardent, W. E.	W
26/293	Private	Schroeder, A.	
10/2763	Private	Simmiss, F. A. H.	D W
23262	Private	Sleath, A. A.	
14695	Private	Storm, L. C.	
26/1723	Private	Stretton, L.	
20581	Private	Tallke, R.	
16009	Private	Taylor, R.	W
25/1022	Private	Spillane, G. J. D.	W
10/4008	Private	Thacker, J.	D W
10406	Private	Thoumine, L. S.	
7/2176	L.-Corporal	Watts, V. A.	W
15826	Private	Wills, S. F.	
10110	Private	Curtis, R. H.	K
11/1414	Private	Brown, J. A.	
3/1381	Private	Byron, A. J. W.	
36718	Private	Clark, G. L.	W
28113	Private	Donaldson, J. D.	W
3/3491	Private	Francis, R. S. R.	
34356	Private	Gibson, F. H.	W
24/703	L.-Corporal	Kemsley, E.	W
1/506	Private	Walker, T. W.	W
18519	Private	Wright, A.	W
12/2088	Private	Price, A.	W
39647	Private	Adams, G.	W
53459	Private	Askey, J. W.	W
45181	Private	Baker, F.	K

W denotes Wounded   D W denotes Died of Wounds
2 W denotes Twice Wounded   D S denotes Died of Sickness
K denotes Killed in Action

134   NEW ZEALAND CYCLIST CORPS

20087	Private	Booth, E. L.	
46164	Private	Borck, C. A.	
47696	Private	Bain, J. J.	
26/1055	Private	Barrett, L. J.	
10/2533	Private	Brightwell, F.	
53120	Private	Binney, T. L.	
59312	Private	Brown, F. F.	
46979	Private	Collinson, A. J.	
44898	Private	Coleman, C. C.	
17696	Private	Clark, J. A.	
37774	Private	Coleman, R. J.	W
62942	Private	Duggan, J. A.	
28692	Private	Dean, C. J.	
6/3003	Private	Dunnill, A. V.	W
24808	Private	Ashby, W. T.	
45486	Private	Davidson, C. A. L.	
52171	Private	Douglas, G. A.	
59342	Private	Egginton, N. A.	W
14084	Private	Edgar, W. C.	
52981	Private	Frederick, S. F.	
39984	Private	Glenn, A.	
57151	Private	Gailer, A. E.	W
38379	Private	Green, W. T.	
36611	Private	Harlwick, G. S. E.	
25525	Private	Hunwick, C. E.	
58876	Private	Hoatten, F. A. P.	
38538	Private	Henderson, J. A.	
31638	Private	Hampson, W. T.	
13016	Private	Hareton, J. E.	K
26832	Private	Hadden, G.	
40952	Private	Hubbard, C.	
22982	Private	Harding, T. R.	
51849	Private	Johnson, W. W.	W
59654	Private	Johnson, H. J.	K
26111	Private	Johnson, A. F.	
38546	Private	Knox, A. D.	W
13/1329	Private	Lindsay, H. J.	K
32524	L.-Corporal	Lorimer, G.	
53037	Private	Lloyd, C. H.	
46736	Private	McKenna, P. J.	W
49197	Private	McKinlay, J. B.	W
19026	Private	McCutcheon, A. J.	

W denotes Wounded   D W denotes Died of Wounds
2 W denotes Twice Wounded   D S denotes Died of Sickness
K denotes Killed in Action

APPENDIX 135

51865	Private	McLeod, A. R.	K
56333	Private	McGoram, E. R.	
11705	Private	McKenzie, K. C.	
28511	Private	Mills, H.	K
47355	Private	McNaul, D.	
57239	Private	McDowall, S.	
53397	Private	Ormand, W. A.	W
47177	Private	O'Connell, B. J.	
33054	Private	Ogilvie, G. E.	
44310	Private	Patter, J. F.	
12/3134	Private	Quarrie, F.	W
51071	Private	Rolls, H.	
9/1613	Private	Ryan, T.	
24492	Private	Robertson, O.	
35220	Private	Reidy, P.	
58932	Private	Shirres, L. E.	
39346	Private	Stewart, D. A.	
31368	Private	Symons, E.	
46397	Private	Smith, F. W. T.	K
47686	Private	Scott, S. C.	W
32401	Private	Sincock, H.	
24081	Private	Topps, W. E.	
6/2785	Private	Twizell, J.	
47486	Private	Vennell, C.	W
46198	Private	Wright, W. O.	
8/2756	Private	Webb, A. R.	
30680	Private	White, L. G.	W
26357	Private	Win, D. W.	
55359	Private	Beal, A. T.	
8/3257	Private	Ferguson, J. A.	W
47138	Private	Harrison, D. E.	W
52242	Private	Meachem, W.	
52477	Private	Smith, E. H.	
12/2948	Private	Begovich, S.	W
9/1382	Private	Bevan, J.	
3/2368	Private	Bolton, F. G.	W
41716	Private	Brosnahan, P. J.	
28981	Private	Cooke, G. W.	W
46878	Private	Doidge, O. J.	
45254	Private	Egan, P. C.	
16214	L.-Corporal	Foote, R. A.	D W
10342	Private	Hagan, C.	W

W denotes Wounded   D W denotes Died of Wounds
2 W denotes Twice Wounded   D S denotes Died of Sickness
K denotes Killed in Action

New Zealand Cyclist Corps

45034	Private	Hurst, S.	W
40312	Private	Gifford, R. H.	W
26308	Private	Oliver, W. R.	
36664	Private	Park, J. G.	
34430	Private	Regan, R. J.	
27618	Private	Shepherd, J.	
34445	Private	Smith, J. G.	
10184	Private	Watkinson, H.	W
10/3438	Private	Woodham, S.	
24264	Private	Woolley, D. S.	
16707	Private	Moore, L. G.	
5/355	Private	Stock, L. N.	W
12213	Private	Laws, C. R.	
10290	Private	Apperley, L. P.	
5/872	Private	Barwick, H.	
23/1554	Private	Bennett, R. G.	
10/2863	Private	Blair, J. W.	
5/277	Private	Boocock, A. F.	W
33821	Private	Brady, F. D.	
28098	Private	Cantwell, H. H.	
12/324	Private	Cavenett, W. G.	
12/329	Private	Chandler, P. H.	
28086	Private	Chapman, G.	
12/2175	Private	Cochrane, W.	
31600	Private	Cook, R. W.	
10/2574	Private	Dale, J. L.	
12/3629	Private	Egan, G.	
10/3254	Private	Elvines, O. L.	
12/1087	Private	Fagan, J. A.	
12/4176	Private	Furber, P.	
11/1317	Private	Gee, R.	
10/3892	Private	Hall, H. C.	W
23/1652	Private	Hall, J. E.	
12/2321	Private	Hastings, W. C.	
10/348	L.-Corporal	Holt, J. W.	W
10/4463	Corporal	Hunter, A. W.	
33370	Private	Irwin, H.	W
10/3613	Private	Johnson, M.	
17/362	Private	Johnson, R.	
9/1576	Private	Jones, A. E.	
11047	Private	Jones, N. L.	
28165	Private	Lewis, A. E.	

W denotes Wounded
2 W denotes Twice Wounded
K denotes Killed in Action
D W denotes Died of Wounds
D S denotes Died of Sickness

APPENDIX

11/2642	Private	Lumsden, J. S.	W
10/3639	Private	Maitland, J. M.	
12230	Private	Metcalfe, H. H.	W
12340	Private	Mills, H.	
13057	L.-Corporal	Mourie, F.	
5/1886A	Private	Mullis, W. W.	
12463	Private	Paddison, H.	
10/4157	Private	Quarrie, F.	
25590	Private	Raby, G. S.	
12/4129	Private	Rattray, S.	
23/1792	Private	Ridling, M. L.	
32076	Private	Shaw, W. F.	
31442	Private	Skelley, A. L.	
29503	Corporal	Smith, P. J.	
12/2486	Private	Taylor, J. F.	
11977	Private	Thomas, C. H.	
25616	Private	Thompson, G.	
12/3847	Private	Tole, H.	
14702	Private	Vold, P. N.	
23459	Private	Warden, H. L.	
13157	Private	White, H.	W
6/4591	Private	Capon, W. J.	
33691	L.-Corporal	Catley, G.	
10125	Private	Currie, W. G.	
8/824	L.-Corporal	Faulkner, J.	W
29875	Private	Hutchinson, W. G.	
8/3324	Private	Lyndon, E. A.	
27945	Private	O'Connell, S. R.	
22082	Corporal	Pearson, L. R.	
9/1485	Private	Rowlands, L. E.	
6/4357	Private	Shaw, J.	
15311	Private	Oliver, A. M.	W
30508	Private	Banks, G.	
11643	Private	Finlay, S.	
10051	Private	Prenderville, M.	
40274	Private	Abdallah, H.	
25436	Private	Balks, J.	
10/2844	Private	Baines, H. O.	
30336	Private	Baker, C. A.	
20291	Private	Bridgeman, N.	
35142	Private	Brookes, H. G.	
24518	Private	Burton, E. J.	

W denotes Wounded   D W denotes Ded of Wounds
2 W denotes Twice Wounded   D S denotes Died of Sickness
K denotes Killed in Action

NEW ZEALAND CYCLIST CORPS

36850	Private	Butler, G. A.	
18199	Private	Connell, T. D.	
25814	Private	Cook, H.	
7/1606	L.-Corporal	Davidson, J. H.	
31236	Private	Death, N. G. A.	
18632	Private	Denham, G.	
25479	Private	Dornauf, A. J.	
34342	Private	Dunwoodie, J. L.	
27079	Private	Elliott, R. E.	
30781	Private	Flavell, E. E.	
31264	Private	Halligan, W. J.	
24/799	Private	Hodges, F.	
11396	Private	Jepson, C. J.	
30597	Private	Johnson, J.	
11833	L.-Corporal	Jones, C. H.	
26861	Private	Laurie, F. N.	
9/1895	Private	Marks, F. W.	
34397	Private	May, N. A.	
11898	L.-Corporal	Montgomery, E.	
25/725	Private	Morgan, F. L.	
26/598	Private	McKay, A. J.	
10/2698	Private	McWhitter, G. W. A.	
20405	Private	Ogle, M.	
10/3693	Corporal	Paget, G. E.	
28211	Private	Read, R. H. K.	
24420	Sergeant	Reid, R. C.	
40649	Private	Sharp, N.	
30412	Private	Smith, A.	
10085	Private	Spencer, W. C.	
31367	Private	Stemp, H. L.	W
23893	Private	Stuart, W. G.	
30662	Private	Taine, R. V.	
14697	Private	Tanner, L. J.	
24/1499	Private	Thompson, E. D.	
31910	Private	Thorpe, J. H.	
10/2775	Private	Twomey, H. J.	
8/959	Corporal	Warren, S.	
29519	Private	Walker, J. M.	
4/1964	Private	Watson, J.	
30679	Corporal	Welsh, J. A.	
28248	Private	Wemyss, C. R.	
25627	Private	Williams, W. E.	

```
  W denotes Wounded         D W denotes Died of Wounds
2 W denotes Twice Wounded   D S denotes Died of Sickness
  K denotes Killed in Action
```

31389	Private	Winkie, J.	
25631	Private	Wylie, F. J. A.	D W
65336	Private	Bright, A. J.	
25536	Private	Jones, A. E.	
10/4497	Private	Walker, R. T.	
3/1722	Private	Sharpe, F. J.	

W denotes Wounded D W denotes Died of Wounds
2 W denotes Twice Wounded D S denotes Died of Sickness
K denotes Killed in Action

WHITCOMBE & TOMBS LIMITED

ONE OF OUR LAST CASUALTIES.
Grave of Pvte. R. D. Walker, at Saultain.

OUR FIRST CASUALTY.
Grave of Corp. C. S. Des Barres,
at Bois Grenier.

GRAVE OF OUR ADJUTANT.
Captain C. A. Dickeson, M.C. at Abeele.
Private Dickeson, brother to the above in rear of cross.

www.ingramcontent.com/pod-product-compliance
Lightning Source LLC
Chambersburg PA
CBHW021842220426
43663CB00005B/372